THE INTELLIGENCE CODE

by

Sherry Anshara

How the QuantumPathic® Energy Method Transformed 14 Lives

QuantumPathic Press®

Printed in the U.S.A.
Published by QuantumPathic Press®, 6701 E. Clinton Street, Scottsdale, Arizona 85254 U.S.A.

You can contact the author at www.quantumpathic.com.

First Edition: December 2016

ISBN: 978-0-9742144-2-9

Book Cover Design by Tamara Parisio

ACKNOWLEDGMENTS

In Heartness to these incredible beings who, through our connected Soul Agreements, openly and bravely, are sharing with you their experiences as they talk the talk and walk the walk on their paths of Involved Conscious Evolution beyond Duality. They are sharing with you their unique journeys of Healing Them Selves by Taking Back Their Power. As unique as you are, you will be able to relate to their challenges and their victories. YOU too will recognize that the Healer of YOU and your life is YOU. Creating and living beyond Duality is now possible. These individuals are the possibilities and potentials that have become the manifested actualizations of REAL HUMANS creating, implementing, manifesting, and actualizing their lives each and every day beyond Duality.

With Heartness, respect, and admiration to Wind Ohmoto, who assisted in editing this message to the world, my sincere appreciation and gratitude to her. And with the deepest gratefulness to Tamara Parisio for her comprehension of the essence of the QuantumPathic® Energy Method so that she could create and design the cover of this book, beautifully depicting the transformation of the male and female human from the black and white Duality Belief Systems to the full vibratory brilliance of clear Consciousness.

With Heartness and thankfulness to each of these individuals, I know in complete confidence and joy that "being", living, and creating one's life consciously beyond Duality is REAL!

Beyond Thanks to…

Amy Rakowczyk
Tom Hamblin
Nancy Shappell
Traci Bogan
Christina Kovalik
John Gangemi
Sue Barnes
Dwight McKee
Al Swimmer
Wind Ohmoto
Donna Sparaco
Marlo Cook
Cindie Hubiak
Bob Wyndelts

Table of Contents

Foreword

by Sherry Anshara

The purpose of this book, *The Intelligence Code*, is for you, the Reader, to experience the experiences of these individuals who so courageously share their lives as they became Conscious. Their experiences show their dedication to "be" beyond the boxes of Duality as they clearly express their Selves as sovereign, sentient beings who are the examples of being, creating, and living from their Inner Truth and not existing in the limitations of Duality.

Through the QuantumPathic® Energy Method, they have come to know their Selves from the inside out. They continue to be Involved Conscious Evolutionary Revolutionaries in their own personal and professional lives, which are one and the same.

They have chosen to go beyond the limited Belief Systems of Duality. They have chosen to express their Selves to the fullest, experiencing life beyond restricted boxes. They have chosen their own ways while participating fully in this world. They are not hampered by Duality's **B**elief **S**ystems of Fear… The B.S. Programs.

They experience life through their own frequency and vibration that resonates to the four steps of being their own God Self:

1. Creating their lives consciously
2. Implementing their lives on purpose with purpose
3. Manifesting clearly what they are choosing to create
4. Actualizing what they are purposefully creating

They experience their lives. They are experiencing the experiences they create to experience each and every day without the head chatter of their computer/brain. They use both their right and left computer/brain as the tool it was meant to be…to organize information only. Through the organization of information, they can clearly discern what information serves them or not. This is the only purpose of the computer/brain for individuals who are

Conscious. When the computer/brain runs the show, dysfunction is the outcome every time. These amazing individuals live, create, and experience their lives through their Heart. The Heart, the highest vibrational field in the human body, is the real brain.

These are ordinary people who are now living extraordinary lives every day. They are in charge of the circumstances of their lives in the moment of all their moments, and they are consciously creating their lives through their Hearts. Their pasts are in the past, where they belong. Their pasts do not influence or affect them, no matter what came before. They comprehend their past experiences without judging them. They comprehend that it is only in the moment that they create the next moment or moments. This moment is what counts. In this moment, they experience the experience happening now without the head chatter. They experience life through the brilliance of their Hearts. This doesn't mean that they don't have challenges. They do. Remember, this is a Duality Earth and Universe which holds frequencies and vibrations of trauma, illness, and dysfunctions of every kind. As Involved Conscious individuals, they know how, when, where, and why they are choosing to participate or NOT!

If they can do it, so can you!

Enjoy your journey
in Heartness, Allness, and Connectedness
that blesses you in all ways always,

Sherry Anshara

The Intelligent Reasons for This Book

by Sherry Anshara

The minute the sperm hits the egg, you are in! You are a Conscious being absorbing all the feelings and emotions of your parents. You experience from your mother's womb the outside world through your mother's and even your father's points of view from their experiences and Belief Systems. In this world we all experience a dimension known as Duality.

The difference in how you experience life is the difference between the frequencies, vibrations, and resonances of clear feelings and dysfunctional emotions. Feelings come from the Heart. The Heart has a vibrational field and frequency that is at least 500 times more expanded than your brain. Emotions and the resultant dysfunctional repeatable patterns come from the left brain.

The left brain, which is connected to the right male "man"-ifesting side of your body, has a very low frequency and vibration. The repeated results are the repeated patterns of behaviors. The left brain and right male side run the Duality do-over programs. The left brain is the culprit of your repeated relationships, repeated patterns of dysfunctional behaviors, and the repetition of your emotional challenges.

The right brain, your creative brain which connects to your female left side, appears most of the time to be dormant, while the left brain is repeatedly dominant. Since we are not taught or shown the difference, feelings and emotions are categorized as one and the same. They are not. The differences between feelings and emotions are significant in how your computer/brain affects how you create your life.

The experiences you experience from your very inception are directly linked to how you create your illnesses, diseases, and relationship trauma dramas that occur as a result of your emotional body. Your experiences from a clear Heart support you to be very powerful and healthy. Your emotional body "supports" you to experience life through the trauma dramas, always seeking validation outside of your Self regardless of what you have accomplished in your idea or not. Your emotional re-actions are the results of Duality. Your Heart-based feelings are your intuitive guidelines. In your emotional computer/brain, life is always challenging. Emotionality is the ups and downs that drive you crazy. In your clear Heart, your life flows as though your particles are soaring on a wave of Consciousness.

What is Duality? Duality is the good and the bad, the high and the low, the this and the that of life. Duality is all the judgments of each other and especially of your Self. Never being good enough! Never really validated! Never, never, never something or other. From the beginning, without judging your parents or family, Duality is a constricting frequency and vibration that resonates to you being confined and limited and always waiting to be happy. Is happiness a temporary figment of Duality's reality?

Whatever Belief Systems of ideas, perceptions, or limitations of your parents and/or grandparents, you are taught to experience your life from what they know and don't know. They have their agendas about what you are to be or to do. You are to be the next generation of their version of Duality's family line. When there is strife, fighting or abuse in the family, the next generation usually perpetuates what happened before. More times than not, your parents followed in your grandparents' footsteps with perhaps the same ideas, the same limitations, the same Belief Systems, the same behaviors, and the same old same old. In the case of adoptions, abandonment, or kicked out of the family, you still carry their programs from the minute the sperm hits the egg and you are in; you will still process their "stuff". The interesting thing is that their "stuff" may not show up for years, but eventually it does.

Duality's teaching for you is to belong to the "perfect" group: politics, religions, social-economic, ethnic, academic, right side, wrong side of the tracks, etc. You are taught from the beginning that you have to "belong" in order to be validated or accepted. You have to fit in! How funny when one of the most challenging emotional issues is the one of not being validated. Years along the timeline of your life are spent trying to fit in, trying to be accepted. Yet one of the greatest emotional hang-ups is just that…not being validated outside of your Self. You are programmed to fit in, which brings about many emotional issues of not fitting in. You are not supposed to be different. Yet many of you reading this book may experience the emotionality of not fitting in your own biological or even adopted family. How many of you are the "black sheep" of the family? Or the different one? Or are you bluntly asked, "Where did you come from?!"

Without judgment or blame, this is the "because" factor or the "Why's" of how your parents influenced and affected your life from the beginning. They just did the best and worst they could with what they knew and didn't know. Mostly it was what they didn't know. They were following some Belief System so they could fit in, and then you, as their offspring, could fit in too. The Truth is…who really fits in? "Fitting-in" is a Duality Belief System. "Fitting-in" is a delusional illusion. Look back, as the Non-Emotional Observer (NEO), to the times in your past when you did fit in and then for some reason you didn't fit in anymore. Was it "them" that cast you out? Or did you cast your Self out and you didn't realize you created being cast out? Is the result of you being cast out an opportunity for you to change, shift, or expand your Self? Or were you too emotional to see the value of being cast out and you did not recognize the opportunity to grow beyond the Belief System of "not fitting-in"?

The emotional issue is that you "thinky-thinky" from your computer/brain that it was all about "them". You did not recognize that it was all about you! Remember, this is not a judgment. This is the way it is in Duality. If you are a good child, they are good parents. If you are a bad child, they ask, "Where did you come from?" The results of your life are directly connected to those formative years of what you were taught about your Self. Get it? What You were taught about Your Self. Rarely, if ever, were you asked what was going on inside of you, what thoughts you had about how you were processing your life. In life's process of Duality, the inner turmoil is the inner fight that is to be expected when you follow someone else's idea of you instead of supporting your Self to progressively process your own inner Self as you journey along your path.

Your results in any given situation along your path are processed through the Duality Programs that are imprinted in you. They are in direct relationship to what you were programmed through the Belief System that influenced your ideas, thoughts, interactions, relationships, marriage(s), careers—virtually every aspect of your life at all your ages and stages. What others imprinted in you, if you were not able to discern for your Self at your young age, you then just had to accept what was said to you about you.

From the beginning, you are imprinted with information. It's how you process the information, in-form-at-ion, which means how you are formed at your ion or cellular level of your Beingness. The information imprinted in you and your cells is how you have learned or been programmed to experience your life from the beginning. How does all this information get imprinted at your ion level or in your cells? As an analogy, your body is like an iPod. It records all your experiences, all the words, all the ideas, all the concepts you are taught.

This imprinting is called Cellular Memory. Your computer/brain doesn't remember all of your experiences. Your body does. Accessing your Cellular Memory as the Non-Emotional Observer (NEO) is an important step to sorting out your past from a clear, objective, non-emotional viewpoint to heal. Without addressing the emotionality of your experiences, you become sick. Billions are spent on ways to heal. Yet people are getting sicker.

The first place to begin healing emotionally, physically, spiritually, mentally, and financially is to connect to your past experiences as the Non-Emotional Observer (NEO). Now listen to what your body has to say. Your body will provide you with your answers when you are not attached to the emotionality of your past experiences. When you do this, you are connected to your Heart; your computer/brain can no longer control you, judge you, and make you sick.

Knowing at my deepest knowing I cannot change the past. What I can do is release the past from the cellular level of my Consciousness where it no longer serves me. As the Non-Emotional Observer, I can see everyone's part in my life, especially my own.

This is where the Contracts become evident. In the past, no one mentioned to me about any Contract? What? The Truth is you did choose your parents, your placement in your biological family or adopted family or no family, and your path. You can call it destiny or fate. They are the same. They are two words, two descriptives, yet the same Duality Program. Guess what? You can change everything…if you choose! As you become more of an Involved Conscious Evolutionary Revolutionary for your Self, destiny and fate are not relevant. Why? Because you are choosing how you create, implement, manifest, and actualize your life. You are in charge of your path!

All Contracts can be changed, deleted, and completed as you become more involved in your Conscious Evolution.

Any Contract can be changed or voided. The problem with Duality is you are supposed to be stuck in one or all of the Karma, Lessons and Re-Incarnation Programs. You don't have to do it. Actually, all three of these are exactly the same programming; just different words that describe the same limiting, repeatable Belief Systems, the B.S. Programs.

You did not come here to live someone else's idea of your life. You didn't come here to be "born" to die, to suffer, to sacrifice, to be less than, to take a back seat to anyone. These are programs. You have the ability, regardless of your circumstances, to rise above the frequency and vibration of Third Dimension's Duality Programs by taking charge of your life. To be controlled by Duality's limitations is to be stifled and blocked. Free your Self from the boxed-in walls of Duality. You can truly break the ingrained habits of limitation.

"What you say makes your day.

You can either make or break your day or life
or someone else's day or life
by the words, language, and vocabulary you speak."

-Sherryism

Everything is about your frequency and vibration and how you resonate. How you resonate to life, relationships, experiences, and your Self depends upon whether you are Conscious or not. Your frequency and vibration is dependent upon whether you are fear-based or in the process of becoming consciously clear of who you are. The more you detach from the Duality Programs of Fear, regardless of when the imprinting began, the more powerful you become.

As a society of humans, we have not been taught that fetuses are absorbing the details of their parents' experiences. This could be a very scary realization! Or not! Perhaps by reading this book, the realizations or the realize with "real eyes" will be the wake-up call that can change the dynamics of the future of this world for every human being. This is a paradigm shift.

This could be The Shift that has been alluded to for many years, if not decades. This is the paradigm shift of Involved Conscious Evolution. Whatever your age or stage of life, you begin in the moment of clarity in which you choose that you have had enough of limitation, enough of Duality's boxes of confinement preventing you from being in your own Power. You now have the opportunity to choose to express your creativity as an Involved Conscious Evolutionary Being. You definitely deserve to have the life you desire and require to have.

Clarity, detachment, and willingness are keys to the Involved Conscious Evolution. Become involved in your own life. Stop looking outside of your Self for the answers. Outside of you are only the Duality Programs which encourage you to deny and question your innate natural abilities to be the God Self within your human Self. You were never meant to be less or live in physical and emotional pain. Duality itself is a program.

How does the shift begin for you? Your Consciousness paradigm shift happens when you begin to question everything. Question without judgment EVERYTHING! Question with the focus that you already have your Truth inside of you! Without judgment or the fear of not fitting in, you do not have to accept the "trues" which you were taught or were programmed into you. You are conditioned to think that what you think are your own thoughts. Until you question, how do you know for sure that what you were taught is really what you are feeling. Even when you knew that these limited Belief Systems did not "feel" correct to you deep inside, you were programmed to accept these limitations as a reality for you. When you are limited, you are very controllable and easily led away from your Self. Remember, from the minute the sperm hits the egg, you are in. You are being conditioned to be controlled and manipulated. You are taught to not be you.

Begin by examining all your Belief Systems. How do you do this? In quantum physics, in order to witness a change, you must become the observer. As the Non-Emotional Observer (NEO), you are not trying to force a change or re-experience the past. As an example, PTSD, Post-Traumatic Stress Syndrome, is the re-experiencing of the trauma emotionally and physically. As the observer, you allow your Self to detach by recognizing the facts of the circumstances. Without the tremendous fears in these experiences, you begin to release and eventually eliminate the emotional attachment to the traumatic events that kept you bound to the past.

Physical and emotional experiences are physical because you are physical. In Candace Pert's book, *Molecules of Emotions*, she describes how neuronets in your brain are established. As an example, you could have been abused as a child or praised as a child. The neuronet in your computer/brain is based upon your experience or experiences. If you are victimized, your neuronet says you are a victim. If you are praised, the neuronet says you are praised. When an experience happens to you, let's say at six years old, you have established a pathway of communication in your brain. Someone says to you at six years old you are "stupid". You experience the imprinting of being stupid in your brain and your body has to go along with this limited Belief System.

Now let's say you are working at your first job at age sixteen. Your supervisor says to you that you did something stupid, maybe not because you did but maybe he or she was having a bad day. You don't know the facts. You can only re-act, re-experience you being stupid by someone else's limitations or restricted ideas. In that moment, regardless of your actual age, you are emotionally six years old. As you go through life, any time you are called stupid, again regardless of age, stage, education, or credentials, emotionally you are always six years old.

Any person who calls a six-year-old stupid is coming from his or her own judgment from his or her past of being called stupid. The neuronet in your brain recognizes an attack. Your brain does not know what time it is. In this moment, you are emotionally six forever. Let's say you make it to the boardroom of a corporation. You are the CFO, Chief Financial Officer, and the CEO, Chief Executive Officer, says your report is stupid. How old are you? What happens is your dormant neuronet re-fires and you are six again. Your brain has no clue how old you really are.

Without judging your past, your parents, the groups in which you participated, and especially your Self, by sticking to the facts, instead of the emotional attachments triggered by your neuronets, you realize with "real eyes" you are not stupid. Perhaps you "bought" the stupid program, but now as an Involved Conscious Evolutionary Revolutionary you can delete this particular "stupid" program. You can take charge of your life. You can imprint in your own neuronets with what makes sense to you.

As an Involved Conscious Evolutionary, examine all the words, sentences, and vocabulary that trigger upsets in you. As soon as you recognize that you are in an unnatural state of emotional upset, take this as an opportunity to connect to your body and your computer/brain. Your body has all the answers. It knows why you are upset. It knows the time and circumstances that upset you. Your computer/brain is the trigger for your upsets.

As you stay the Non-Emotional Observer (NEO), you will get your answers clearly. With the answers and all the information imprinted in you, you can now begin clearing the non-productive, non-functional, emotional, and repeatable neuronets in your computer/brain. You do not unconsciously have to be stuck in your dysfunctional past continuing to be re-triggered over and over again. Clearing those disabling neuronets frees you to create fun, functional, and productive neuronets for your Self.

FREE YOUR NEURONETS!

In the Chaos that Is Occurring Now

by Sherry Anshara

We have never had this level of technology before. We are getting information as it unfolds. But we also are getting information that is filtered through Belief Systems.

And when we get information that is filtered through these Duality Belief System (B.S.) Programs, we are not always clear on the facts. Though it may appear factual in the media, it is still filtered. And whoever it is that is filtering it—the government or the news media or however they are disseminating the news—they disseminate it with the frequency and vibration of fear. And fear is lack of information.

Because we have this technology, we are getting what looks like minute-to-minute blows of what is going on. However, we still don't have the actual facts. Is there a possibility of cover-up? Is there a possibility of manipulating the population into fear? Sometimes propaganda can manipulate us into a frenzy of fear.

And fear can make people do things that are completely irrational because they don't have the facts. Here's a case in point. After 9/11 in Arizona, a man was murdered because someone thought he was a Muslim. This was not about Christian-Muslim. This is really about people. Someone murdered a man who happened to be a Sikh. He was Indian. Because he had his turban on, the person who did it was taking revenge in his idea. In the fear, irrational and illogical behavior can happen when we don't have the facts.

In my own experience, I believe in research to find out what is going on. I look at all the different views. One of the tools of the QuantumPathic® Energy Method is to be NEO, a Non-Emotional Observer, so we can observe all of the information without any emotional attachments. We simply observe all of the behavior that is occurring around the issues. By doing this and by being NEO, the client does not have to jump back into an emotional frenzy based upon his or her dysfunctional past.

Therefore, the chaos that you are experiencing, emotionally and physically, is the upset frequency and vibration that you continue to resonate from your computer/brain through your body which manifests in your outside world. Unconscious chaos actualizes frenzied turmoil in your life and in your body. Chaos, whether unconscious or even subconscious, causes all sorts of illness, relationship problems, as well as financial issues.

What can you do with this chaos? The question really to ask your Self is…"Why am I allowing chaos to run my life?" One possible reason is that you get "hooked" on the emotional hit. It gives you a false high, and then the let-down comes. As this re-cycle phenomenon occurs, your body eventually breaks down. This can be defined as a mental, an emotional, a spiritual, and even a financial break-down in your life. What you may not be able to "see" is that a break-down, regardless of what you call it, is all physical. Why? Because you are a physical being. All of these definitions are aspects of how you are processing your own life and how you are creating your life, whether you are Conscious of all of it or not. So the issue is…do you decide to continue Self-created chaos or do you choose consciously Self-created stability?

"You are a human being having multi-dimensional experiences.

It is how you choose to have your experiences,
emotionally, mentally, physically, spiritually, and financially."

Here is the caveat. Everyone seems to say this statement when they are avoiding their Selves or avoiding "healing" their issues…"I am not ready!" The Truth is it's not about being ready. It's all about being willing. It is your willingness that will change the dynamics whether you heal or not. Please understand that the issue has nothing to do with you being ready. Unless you are *willing*, you will continue to be at a standstill locked in your past. At this point, your emotional, mental, physical, spiritual, and financial issues will stay stuck in your body as you are stuck in your past.

A possible first step is to consider connecting to your own body. Most people, whether they are aware of it or not, are out of body. A simple example, have you ever driven somewhere and you can't remember how you got there? Well! You are out of your body and not connected to it. If you have been abused in the past, in childhood or whenever, you are most likely not connected to your body. Have you ever said you feel like you are in a movie? Or, do you experience life from the outside looking in? These are significant aspects of being out of body.

When you are out of body, you are not connected. Not only are you not connected to your Self, you are not connected to the world outside of you. It does indeed appear as though you are going through the motions. Do you ever remember saying that to your Self or to someone else? Therefore, connecting to your body is for sure an initial step to getting grounded and feeling alive. At this point, you are clearly initiating the progressive process of being really alive. Isn't that why you came here to Earth...to be alive? Going through the emotions is unnatural.

"What is your purpose?
There is no one purpose. You have many purposes.
You can't know one or any purpose if you are not fully alive."

Another step to consider is to determine where you are experiencing the physical and emotional problems, issues, or illnesses in your body. Ask your Self, what are you experiencing? Can you describe what your body is telling you? Or are you too much in your head to connect to your body? As long as you stay in your head, you will never connect to your body. Your computer/brain can only compute fear!

"Fear is lack of information.
It is NOT false evidence appearing real."

In order to alleviate your fear or fears, you must connect to the cellular intelligence and intellect within your body. Since your body is imprinted with all the experiences you have ever had in your continuum, what better place to find your answers? Your body is an encyclopedia of you. By accessing this information, as you become the Non-Emotional Observer (NEO), you find your answers without the emotionality attached to your experiences. From this vantage point, you can see your part in your experiences as well as the others in your life without blame, shame, guilt, or whatever, and you can begin to heal your past issues without re-traumatizing your Self. Getting the information from your body happens easily when you stay non-emotional and observe the situations, experiences, and events. When you acknowledge and accept that all of your experiences are Self-created, you definitely begin to heal your Self. You are now beginning to step into your Power, as these participants in this book have done.

"As you step into your Self-Power,
some wonderful things begin to happen in your Self-created life.

The blame stops, the guilt stops, the Duality Programs begin to dissipate,
and productive creativity begins."

Now, as you begin the progressive process of being an Involved Conscious human being, as your internal chaos turns into productive stability, you are not as easily influenced by the outside world chaos. You will not be as affected by the media as they propagate all of the Duality Fears and the separation-from-each-other programs.

One of the purposes of the Duality Fear Programs is to keep you separated from your Self. When you are afraid of your own Power, you are easily manipulated to be separated from others. It is also so easy to keep you separated from those within your own family. Why?

The reason is you are programmed to label each member of your family. When they do not "fit" into the labeled boxes, mother, father, sister, brother, grandparents, etc., the Disney boxes that you have been conditioned to place them in, conflict reigns. As this happens, you may not be aware that you are also being placed in a Disney box of their idea about you, and…you wonder as they do what is going on!

What is going on is that everyone, including you, are trying and trying and trying to fit into the labels. As a result, profiles and behavioral patterns are then established. Everyone has a profile of how they are expected to act in the relationship. As these behavioral patterns are established, everyone gets stuck in a role. A role that is defined by the unreal realities of Duality.

Ask your Self, are you a label, a role, a behavioral pattern, and a profile established by someone else's idea of you? Could this be a reason why you have experienced being different from everyone in your family? Could it be a reason why you experience being disconnected from not only your Self but others? Are you the "black sheep" of the family or are you the paradigm shifter that has not been recognized?

Perhaps chaos is your new friend. Could it be, at this time on this planet in this moment, you are becoming consciously Conscious that Duality is not real? You may connect to one or to all of these individuals in this book as they share their own personal journeys out of Duality as they continue to live in their Hearts through Heartness each and every day. Does it mean their lives are perfect? What is perfect? What they are doing is making Conscious choices to comprehend their own roles in their lives. They are also aware of the profiles of the people in their lives and they are better equipped to participate with them more consciously through their clear awareness. Their behaviors are more effective and productive. They "practice" being NEO, Non-Emotional Observers.

Does chaos outside of them affect them? Perhaps yes. But more likely, NO. They are clearly aware that they are in charge of their lives. They are Conscious that they are creating every aspect of their lives. They are more fully engaged in their own lives and in their relationships to their Selves, their families, their friends, even their co-workers. They are living examples of the QuantumPathic® Energy Method. Chaos does not have to rule your life. As you move beyond Duality in this lifetime, you recognize, as these individuals have, that as a Sovereign Being, you are in charge of your life. As a Conscious Creator, you now create, implement, manifest, and actualize your life. Through clear Conscious choices that can be changed or expanded as you are in your Power, you are living you.

"Your outside world is not a reflection.
Your outside world is a projection of you."

-Sherryism

NEW BEGINNINGS

"Love…

How you love makes the difference.

Love fully and your life is full!"

-Sherryism

Welcome, Anya

by Amy Rakowczyk

Back in 2008, my husband and I decided we were ready to start our family. Like most couples, we believed that within a month or two we would be pregnant and starting our journey as parents. Unfortunately, things did not work out that way for us. Many months went by with nothing happening. We started to worry that something was "wrong". We started reading books about conceiving and eventually sought out help from an infertility doctor.

I was diagnosed with endometriosis and was told that it would be near to impossible for me to have a baby on my own. I would need medical intervention. That particular doctor handled things with a sort of "Cut to the Chase" mentality, and before we knew it, I was on ovulating medication and set up for an IUI (intrauterine insemination).

After the treatment, my body responded with a terrible allergic reaction and it was unsuccessful in achieving pregnancy. At this point, we knew that my body was not going to respond well to fertility medications and procedures. We either had to find another way, or we would try to adopt a child.

This began my journey into discovering alternatives to my traditional ways of viewing health and treatment of disease. I changed my diet and sought help from an acupuncturist, hoping that would help us conceive. Within three months, I was pregnant.

Unfortunately, that pregnancy ended in miscarriage, leaving us incredibly heart-broken, but still hopeful. I WAS able to get pregnant. My body could do it.

Sadly, after that loss, we had several other early losses, and hope was diminishing again. At this point, we moved to a new city due to my husband's career, and I found Dr. Kanodia through the Ohio State University Center for Integrative Medicine.

At our first meeting, Dr. Kanodia referred me immediately to Sherry Anshara to address my anxiety. He instructed me to take three phone sessions with her, and when I felt ready, he would put me on a specialized diet to get my body and mind in balance.

I honestly did not realize I had anxiety. I have always been this way, so I thought everyone was like this! It turns out I was living with moderate-to-severe anxiety.

My first appointment with Sherry Anshara was on December 6, 2012 and was unlike anything I had ever experienced before. It was like she was able to dive through all the layers of my conscious and subconscious mind, and find the root of what was ailing me. It was enlightening and transforming.

First she asked me a series of questions very quickly, wanting me to answer with my initial gut feeling before thinking about the question. The strangest answers started coming out—strong answers but almost like they belonged to someone else. She then asked me to repeat some phrases after her to help create a new dialogue. I hung up from that conversation not sure of what happened and thinking, "That was weird. But that was powerful."

A few days later, I was driving home from work when a memory from the past, one that I had not thought about in a very long time, rose up from the depths and presented itself to me. "How strange," I thought. It was like I was remembering it without re-living the pain of it. A little moment frozen in time.

During my next session with Sherry Anshara, I told her about the memory and she immediately saw that experience as a defining moment in my life. She said, "You are afraid of being abandoned and you are afraid that you might abandon your child. I'd like you to repeat after me: I will not be abandoned. I will not abandon my child."

Believe me that this hit me like a tons of bricks. The truth of this statement was so overwhelming that I could barely utter the words. But I did, and I kept uttering them until a new truth arose in me. It's hard to describe, but I just knew, "March. March is when my child will come."

I started the diet Dr. Kanodia recommended and continued the work Sherry Anshara taught me on freeing myself of my belief systems and taking my power back. I kept reminding myself to free myself of the past, and that the stories in my head weren't true. My fears could be relieved by telling myself that I would not be left by my loved ones, and that I would be there for my child. I was loved and I was ready to be a mother.

In February, I woke from a sleep. I had dreamt of my daughter. I saw her face, her long dark hair, and big eyes. She knew I was ready and I knew she was ready.

On March 3, 2013, I took a pregnancy test, the most relaxed one I had ever taken, because I already knew what it would say. I was pregnant. I was going to bring this beautiful little girl into the world.

At the end of March, my husband and I had two more phone appointments with Sherry Anshara to connect with our growing baby. I told her that I felt very strongly that I was having a girl. She agreed and said that the baby felt very strong. We connected with her and started our relationship right away. It was beautiful!

Throughout my pregnancy, I talked to my daughter daily, telling her that she was strong, healthy, brilliant, and beautiful – guided by the teachings and advice from Sherry Anshara. I told her that we were honored to be her caregivers and we fully welcomed her into our lives.

I had a few more dreams of her, one where she told me what her name was. We decided that we would give her a new name and asked for her blessing. There was no protesting that we sensed!

I still experienced some anxiety during the pregnancy because I had several situations that were risk factors for pre-term labor. The main focus of my whole pregnancy was to keep the baby in there as long as possible!

On one occasion when I was about five months along and feeling especially concerned, I heard her tell me, "Mom, I love you. I'm fine." It was unexpected, incredible, and reassuring. I was able to relax after that!

As it turns out, my due date—November 26, 2013—came and went. She was still waiting for the right time. As the days ticked by, it came time to set an induction date, which I postponed as long as was allowed. It was set for December 10th.

Whether it is a coincidence or something unexplainable, I went into labor and gave birth to my daughter exactly a year, to the day, after the first appointment I had with Sherry Anshara — December 6, 2013.

Our daughter was born completely awake and alert, with eyes wide open, taking it all in. She knew me right away and knew her dad's voice. Whenever he spoke she would react, showing a bit of excitement. From the beginning, she would stare deep into our eyes. It was like we had already known each other for a long time.

As I reflect back on the last couple of years, my understanding of the world has changed greatly. I truly believe that we all are conscious from the very beginning. Life is miraculous and mysterious! I am incredibly grateful that my path crossed with Dr. Kanodia and Sherry Anshara. I believe through their guidance and care, I was able to open up and allow my daughter to find her way through.

Parenting and the Power of Being NEO

by Tom Hamblin

I was nervous when my future foster son and I met for the first time in the living room of his group home. He was 12. I was 52. "Hi Dad," he said immediately. Instead of being touched, I wondered, "Why did he address me this way without knowing me? Is he manipulating me? I have been down this road before."

I'd always felt called to be a parent. But I'd been burned. Five years earlier, my relationship had ended that I felt was surely leading in the direction of marriage and, though at a later age than most, a family. I was single again and had some health issues. I signed up for foster/adoptive parent classes. Then I became a foster parent to a boy who tortured my beloved dogs and set fire to my house. I tried everything to make it work—even sending one of my dogs away—but Trevor (not his real name) was too much for me to handle alone.

This time when the social worker from the agency I'd previously worked with called and said, "I have your kid," I said, "No you don't."

It's interesting how the Universe conspires to get you where you are meant to be. I'd just discovered the QuantumPathic® Energy Method (QPEM) and started taking classes that same week. If Sherry Anshara hadn't talked about what it means to manifest, I may have not recognized one of the most important experiences of my life.

I realized I had already done everything leading up to a manifestation. I had set in motion everything required to become a parent, taking classes for a year, passing background checks, and letting friends and family know of my intent to become a dad. I could see in that phone call that all I had to do was say "yes" and *Voila!* I would be a parent. So I did. I changed my "No, you don't" to a "Yes, I will." That "Yes" allowed the manifestation of my lifelong dream, although my heart wasn't fully in it due to the previous disastrous experience of fostering.

As soon as I felt like he was manipulating me by calling me Dad in our very first moment together, I took out my QPEM toolkit and became NEO, the Non-Emotional Observer. I backed off, got out of my emotions. I physically relaxed, disengaged from my fearful thoughts and emotions, and then visualized myself re-engaging through the heart.

I'm glad I did. Nearly a year later, he revealed that two weeks before he met me, he saw my face in a dream. "When you walked in, I knew who you were. I knew you were my family."

It was a road sign, one of many that told me I was on the right track. Another one was timing. I met him Dec. 16th, 2010, and in synchronicity, my job ended Dec. 17th. It had been outsourced to the Philippines. Fortunately, I was given a fantastic severance.

You have to spend so many hours together before a foster child can move into your home. Because my time was free, we spent every day together. He was able to move into my home in two weeks rather than the required two months.

He was a good kid but his behavior was erratic. I could tell he was very depressed. He was disrespectful, mouthy and blunt. No matter what I said, he bit my head off. I didn't know what to do. Again, fortunately, as difficult as that period was, I had a good toolkit from which to draw. The QuantumPathic® Energy Method (QPEM) kept me sane.

For over a year, every time I got on the phone, he became very needy/wanty, constantly interrupting me. I'm not a yeller. I'm pretty laid back. But this one time I was ready to explode. "Enough! No more!" I said to him. His eyes got really big, like he thought, "Oh, I'm going to get it now."

Before I hung up the phone, I determined I'd remain NEO, the Non-Emotional Observer. Instead of yelling, I put my hand on his cheek, kneeled down and said, "I'm here for you. Just because

I'm talking to other people doesn't mean I don't love you. This doesn't mean I have disconnected from you."

Typically, he wouldn't listen because he would be so agitated, but we had a good talk.

Being the Non-Emotional Observer is not a suppression of emotions. It's a conscious choice to step back, relax, and experience calmness. I LOVINGLY accept and acknowledge my emotions. Then I forgive myself for those times when I allowed my emotions to rule. I acknowledge that in these moments they do not support me to be my best. My emotions then melt away and my feelings become pronounced. Then I act with love through my heart, rather than with anger through my head. What works for me may not work for someone else. Everyone knows best how to get out of their heads and into their hearts. It takes practice.

There was another instance where I felt real brilliance in the moment. He was prone to meltdowns. Screaming, raging, irrational sentences, temper tantrums, demanding, Oppositional Defiance Disorder. When I responded to one of his meltdowns by restricting his Internet use, he flew into an absolute rage. I said, "Calm down or you'll get no Internet." It got worse. He screamed louder, became more irrational, demanding, and disrespectful. "Okay, no Internet for two days." He got worse. "Okay, a week."

I followed him up to his room as he screamed in my face. "I don't understand why you are continuing to do this," I said. "It seems like you want more restrictions." He screamed even louder.

"So why are you doing this to yourself?" I asked, remaining calm and staying NEO, coming from a place of the heart, not the thinky thinky brain.

His eyes flashed. Something magical, something spiritual happened. Immediately he calmed down. In a split moment he realized it wasn't about control at all. It was about him being in charge. He got that he was completely in charge of how restricted he was.

That was the beginning of a big turn for him. After that he began to really calm down. He began to learn about himself and understand for the first time that he was far more in charge of his behavior and thus his life, than he previously had understood.

Eventually, he was diagnosed as Asperger's. Today Asperger's is no longer officially a diagnosis. It is a part of Autism Spectrum Disorder (ASD). At first, though, all I saw was random aggression and fits of lack of self-control. After he'd been with me for a while, I began to notice he did things in kind of an order. He carried a lot of pictures from his childhood adventures in foster care. In photos of himself around age seven or eight, his smile looked very contrived. I thought, "Oh well, he's had a lot of trauma." He'd bounced around a lot of foster homes since he was six years old.

It was a little risky, but I said, "Your smile doesn't seem real. Were you just unhappy? In all those photos, why doesn't your smile look natural?"

"Dad," he said. "I didn't know how to smile. They had to teach me how to smile."

He'd been diagnosed with ADHD and PTSD and many other syndromes with long letters. He was taking medications which did nothing for his behavior. I suspected that his diagnoses weren't correct either.

He was extremely bright, but he was so black and white in his thinking. He'd ask me what time it was. If I said it was 7:30, he'd come back to me very angry. "Dad, you didn't tell me the truth. It's 7:28, not 7:30."

He could not handle humor. He could not understand nuance or the abstract part of a joke. He just did not get it. I began to realize this might be Autism.

Interestingly, since my 20's, information about Autism had fallen into my lap. Although I was in business, I somehow ended up taking classes in holistic health—one of them about the psychology of Autism. The smile conversation triggered the memory of everything I'd learned before. I began to read everything I could about Autism. The more I began to view him with that perspective, the more I saw how that pattern fit him. But he'd been to a psychiatrist who said, "Oh, perfectly typical kid." I knew that was 1,000% incorrect.

During the first several years he seemed on the edge of aggression. I felt compelled to lock up my steak knives and lock the bedroom door at night. "If you strike out at me or the dog, I won't be angry," I told him. "I'll simply call 911. The choice will be entirely yours."

Then he had a particularly violent outburst with a family member. I called 911.

The police picked him up and took him to the juvenile detention center. Typically, for minors, a court hearing is set for the next day. The Judge talks about what happened, gives the youth a sentence or assignment, then releases him into the custody of his parents. My parents happened to be visiting at the time. I did not desire that he come home then because my parents did not have time to pack up their belongings and leave.

The State of Arizona had done us a huge disservice. We never received the services they promised us. I required respite, time away. Parenting him was taxing. We were bound to one organization with a person who did not properly diagnose his condition. He had to have a diagnosis. It was vital I knew what was going on with him so I could tailor my parenting style accordingly.

Knowing all that, I chose to go up against the State of Arizona by myself. Utilizing the QuantumPathic® Energy Method (QPEM) techniques allowed me to stand in my power, and it prevented me from second guessing myself or my choices. In court, the Judge addressed him as he was in handcuffs. "I'm going to hand you over to your father." It was sad to see. Despite his behavior, he was young, very sweet and an innocent, beautiful child.

I raised my hand. "Yes?" said the Judge. "Parents don't speak in here."

I said, "Excuse me, but this parent will speak in here. It is important for you to understand some things. I will not be taking him home today. My parents are still in my home. We keep going in circles here. We have these incidents and it's not getting better. We're not getting the services we require."

"You are remanding your child to the State of Arizona," said the Judge. "You may be brought up on charges of child neglect and abandonment."

By 5:00 that night I had the State of Arizona bearing down on me. "You come get him right now. He's your child. You're in contempt. We'll take him away from you."

I had adopted him several years prior to this court appearance. I was not told of his behavioral issues, or at least they were very glossed over when I did accept him into my home. I was told that a loving home would make all the difference in him. When, in fact, it didn't! Because he was never properly diagnosed.

I said, "You try that. You have failed him and you have failed me. He will come back into the home when you meet the promises you initially made us. We are struggling. That kid is mentally and emotionally on the edge. I place the responsibility upon you."

He moved into a boys' home while I spent three weeks at Child Protective Service (CPS) offices, trying to negotiate. I contacted the attorney who'd handled his adoption. She had great information. She told me exactly what CPS's strategies were and what I could do.

Fear is a lack of information. The QuantumPathic® Energy Method (QPEM) says information is being imprinted as in-form at the ION or cellular level within the body. I being was informed at my ION level. To be informed at the ION level is to have all the necessary details nailed down and comprehended. I had done everything in my power to support him. Understanding this, I could relax and let things happen without FORCING any outcomes. That is important. I was able to play hardball without being emotional, standing in my truth from my ION level of clear awareness.

Within three weeks, I got an appointment with a well-known psychiatrist familiar with Asperger's. I'd been attempting to get an appointment with him for a whole year. He absolutely loved him. By the third visit, the psychiatrist said, "Mr. Hamblin, your son is not just Asperger's. He is a classic, <u>textbook</u> Asperger's."

Then I had to deal with my emotions of anger. My son had been in CPS care for six years prior to coming into my home. He had never received the quality care he deserved.

The psychiatrist put him on medication, which we have since stopped using. It was part of a plan. Through the QuantumPathic® Energy Method (QPEM), I learned that much of who we are, how we act, and even the disease process itself is a profile. I accepted the profile of Asperger's. Then I set out to find ways to get around it. If we are unable to fully get out of the profile, how much of the profile can we fully retire?

Medication was a necessity at that time. I blessed the medication. It calmed him down. It changed his life. It was like all the rust and corrosion had broken away. There is this beautiful kid inside. He still viewed things in black and white, but he could now handle not understanding what people were saying to him. Or even what I was saying to him. In the past, this had been a source of tremendous frustration for him.

He began to realize, "This is what it's like to be calm." For the first time, he knew what calmness felt like in his body. We eventually got him off the medication. Now, without his medication, his behavior continued to be calm, stable, and he appeared more secure.

One of the ways I supported him to let go of his wanty-needy profile and his dependency on medication was teaching him coping skills and sharing with him what I had learned about being more conscious. I learned early on that my role as his parent was to support him in his journey. I have a contract with him and must fulfill my contract as flawlessly as possible.

I began to get involved in organizations and saw how other parents handled their kids. There are a lot of aware people out there who are doing a lot of cool things for their kids with Asperger's. I enrolled him into classes and counseling for his Asperger's.

After five years of negotiating, demanding, and pleading with the school system, I was finally able to get a 504P, which allows various accommodations, such as having more time to take tests and having more access to his teachers. That has been a very good thing for him.

I began to talk to him more in black and white, and then we would stretch. We would stretch a nuance into a little tiny area of gray.

He loathed it, but he got used to it. "Son," I'd always say. "Home is where you get all the wonderful tools you require to live successfully in the world. I'll have to give you a few extra tools that have to do with Autism and Asperger's. I realize you're frustrated. We're stretching you just a little bit, but the world will stretch you just a little bit more. We have to get you prepared for that."

Today at 17, we have wonderful conversations. I don't joke with him. He still does not enjoy that, but he talks to me in ways I never dreamed he would.

There's no doubt we were meant to be father and son. Life can be very deceiving. Someone comes into your life. It seems random, but once you step back, you see all the profound synchronicities that connected you. In Arizona, a CPS committee matches a foster child with an adoptive home. A CPS committee chose me over a family that had previously successfully adopted a special needs child. Because, in the past, I had given up my dog in an attempt to save my first foster child. They knew I would stick with him.

My own life lined up in such a way that I had information about Autism stewing inside that my son and I would one day require. I was single with no other kids to tend and able to give him 100% of my attention. There really was no one else at that point in time and space that could have assisted my son in getting where he is today, five years since we met.

Now the QuantumPathic® Energy Method (QPEM) tools I use have become a part of me. When tough times pop up, I know how to frame things. How to see things as they really are and not how they appear to be. I am still learning, though. We're all mortal. I call myself a work in progress. I'm not perfectly calm or perfect in my parenting skills, but I'm certainly able to improve day by day how I respond to my son.

Like Sherry Anshara says, "You can't get to the *What* until you've uncovered the *Why*." One thing has to precede the other. We uncovered THE ROOT OF HIS BEHAVIOR and then worked **it** forward.

There have been many times that he has hit a wall. But now he focuses on why he does what he does. He feels what he has done is wrong and will apologize. Many Asperger's kids struggle to develop empathy. He is making tremendous progress in this area. He doesn't grow like most kids—at an angle. He grows horizontally. He hits a wall, elevates and then goes again. But he grows nonetheless. He's such a sweet kid, a really good kid.

My friend who is a physician and knows my son very well, now says, "He's just like you." I've been told, I'm kind of chill or, in esoteric terms, serene. My son began to take these qualities on, being his own version of NEO, the Non-Emotional Observer.

One unexpected revelation of parenthood is that a child will not only absorb the habits that are not so favorable, but also emulate the supportive ones that we teach them. When they do, you look at them and see yourself in a very pleasing way.

I am so much freer than the old fettered and tired Tom. Life has more meaning and the experience of it is richer.

RISING ABOVE ABUSE

"If you do not like the issue,

then cancel your subscription and move on!"

-Sherryism

Post-Traumatic Stress Disorder

by Nancy Shappell

Spells. That's what my family called it. My mother called me kooky, friends called me weird, and doctors said I was just imagining things. What kept me stuck? I bought into all of it, believing they were right. And that was the kookiest thing of all.

From my earliest memory at age five until I moved out of the family home at age twenty-two, I experienced sexual molestation in my house. I lived in fear. It was my normal. Things that my heart and mind could not make sense of buried their way into every cell of my body. Those things I fought so hard to keep hidden, my body would never forget. Words, thoughts, and actions slowly grew disease in every secret pocket of my being. They told me I was without worth. If the people who were supposed to love and protect me disrespected me in that way, maybe everyone would.

As a child, while teachers drilled the class in math, science, and history facts, I numbed out to all of it. My academic grades had no significance in my survival. When a child finds herself in a classroom just hours after being raped, learning multiplication tables is non-important. By the time I was in high school, I had disappeared into drugs and alcohol. Years blew by in muted detail.

As an adult, my dissociative seizure-like episodes became crippling. Dizzy spinning, ear humming, teeth grinding, spells that transported me out of my body to places I did not want to re-visit. Trauma had worm-holed deep into my cellular memory. My body shook. My eyes went blank. I groaned and whined and saw my perpetrator grabbing for me. During my full-blown episodes, I knew nothing but fear as I hid under furniture like a beaten dog. Sometimes it was my son's voice I heard begging for me to come back. Comforting me and telling me I was thirty-five years old, the year was 1990, and I was safe in our home. No twelve-year-old should ever be subject to that kind of responsibility.

I was unable to hold a full-time job, properly parent my children, or be a present wife. During the day I was paralyzed in depression. At night I stayed awake in fear of being attacked in the dark. I never felt safe. I never felt believed. I was always physically sick. It was all-consuming for me, my husband, and my two sons. It was our normal.

When I was diagnosed with PTSD, post-traumatic stress disorder, to me it meant nothing other than my life had been compacted and defined by four letters of the alphabet. There were doctors, therapists, hospitalization, and none of it got to the real bottom-line issue. I had a diagnosis. I had more drugs. It felt like the professionals had jumped into the middle of the story, oblivious as to how to heal the root of my issues. I saw myself as a dying plant. Each week I sat in a doctor's office as he picked the dead leaves off me. Then I would feel better for a few hours. But by the next week, what little growth I had gained was dead, and again I was back to where I had started. I had been poisoned. Toxic sludge from fear saturated my roots and it was killing me.

In the summer of 2007, after an autoimmune disease diagnosis, my body was so full of illness I began a year-long regimen of chemotherapy and steroid drugs. Every day I swallowed a fat yellow tablet, lied to myself, and called it sunshine, hoping it would make me well. It never did. In fact, by the end of that year I was more toxic than ever. On my last appointment with the rheumatologist, I told him I was done with doctors and drugs. He leaned back in his chair, stuck one hand in his lab coat pocket, and said, "Well, who do you think is going to manage your health care now?" "I am," I said. "I am sick of being sick."

My inner wisdom was telling me there was a natural way to heal my mind, body, and spirit, and I was going to find it.

I searched the internet for alternative healing modalities. I read dozens of websites. None of them completely clicked with me, until I came across the QuantumPathic® Center of Consciousness. Each word I read connected to my heart. Each paragraph spoke truth.

I listened to Sherry Anshara's radio show, read her first book, *The Age of Inheritance*, and I called the Center and spoke to Sherry Anshara directly. Convinced that this common sense method of healing would teach me to release the fear that had overtaken my whole life, I made an intention to manifest a trip from New England to Arizona. I printed out the course information for Intuitive Powers/Practical Applications I and pasted it to my vision board. Every day I read Sherry Anshara's words. I began feeling stronger and clearer. Months later, I boarded a plane in New Hampshire and flew to Phoenix. Looking out that plane window and down at the city, I felt no fear, only excitement. I was about to change my life.

That first visit to the QuantumPathic® Center of Consciousness in May 2009 fell on the weekend of my fifty-fourth birthday. It was the most loving and valuable gift I could have ever given myself. I made three more visits over the next two and a half years, completing the full courses of Intuitive Powers/Practical Applications I, II, and III, and also participating in several other classes offered there.

What I learned at the QuantumPathic® Center of Consciousness was that all my addictions resonated the same fear. I had been addicted to the need for validation. I had been searching for worth. The emotional hooks to my past and the need to be loved and validated by the very people who abused me had kept me stuck in the old paradigm. My own denial and self-doubt was a continuation of that abuse. As a child, I had fragmented my life experiences because that was the only way I knew to survive. As an adult that fragmentation and lack of Consciousness was what I used for coping skills.

I had spent my life looking for validation somewhere other than within myself. I feared I had no control. I feared I was not worthy of love. Every fear was a road-block to healing. Fear kept me ill. I had hooked into belief systems that were never mine. My outside world had been created by my inside fears. How I saw myself had set me up for the drama in my life.

At the QuantumPathic® Center of Consciousness, I learned to become the non-emotional observer by cutting the bands of shame and blame. I now understood I had choice in my own empowerment or destruction, and it had been my child-self that had been running the show based on my wounded-victim program. And that only invited the trauma drama to be re-created over and over.

Life is wonderful now. I no longer suffer from dissociative spells. There is no longer a need to slip away to that numbing unconscious state. It's been a gradual process of gaining confidence, management of my emotions, letting go of the fear when I felt a dissociative episode coming on, and knowing, what happened years ago, is in the past. Understanding this has been incredibly empowering and validating.

Today I create my life in the most healing and loving ways. I live in respect and celebration of me. I have released toxic emotional and physical pain from my body. I believe I am of worth, deserve to be loved, and enjoy good health.

Living consciously. It is who I am. It is who I choose to be in the evolution of my soul. I have given my feelings a voice and it has been incredibly cathartic. I have changed the way I define myself, thus changing the way I see my world. There is purpose and beauty in that. This is truth. Without truth, there cannot be healing.

I am grateful to Sherry Anshara for facilitating that authenticity in me. The ability to create, implement, and manifest what I require, desire, and deserve.

Nancy Shappell
Author of *A Voice in the Tide: How I Spoke My Truth in the Undertow of Denial and Self-Blame.*
www.nancyshappell.com

Victim to Thriver: Crossing the Threshold of Childhood Sexual Abuse

by Traci Bogan, Dreampreneur

After only 11 minutes of the QuantumPathic® Energy Method (QPEM), I had the single most profound release and breakthrough I've ever experienced around the issues of being sexually abused as a child. Those 11 minutes were worth more than all the tens of thousands of dollars I'd spent for a decade on therapy and every kind of anti-depressant, A-Z. This was at a free introductory lecture! I'd heard about it only 24 hours earlier from someone I'd just met and I felt drawn to go.

I walked in and sat in the front row. Without even a hello, Sherry Anshara walked up to me and said, "You have Hashimoto's disease." True. I did have the autoimmune disorder. But how did she know at first glance, I wondered? "I can see it in your neck," she said. "Would you like to know why you created that for yourself?"

Seriously?? I thought to myself. I was puzzled! She said I was sexually abused as a child and didn't have a voice to speak my truth, thereby creating Hashimoto's disease, TMJ, and chronic back pain. She stated, "Every ache and pain is your body attempting to talk to you. Pay attention. Every piece of illness is your body attempting to talk to you. Most of the time we just don't listen. We cover up the pain with Band-Aids and medicate ourselves to death. Now, are you ready to release this, Traci?"

Yes, I was ready! She was right. I was sexually abused as a child from age 5 until 14. I had what seemed like a lifetime of keeping that silence inside me. It was my dirty little secret. I always felt inadequate and used to pray at bedtime every night for God to make me "normal".

Then somewhere around the age of 20, I told my best friend, Amy. She said I shouldn't have to bear the weight of this on my shoulders any more. I didn't do anything wrong. One day, I picked up the phone and called one of the two uncles who were my perpetrators and said, "I remember what you did to me. I want you to acknowledge it and I want an apology." I can still hear his words and remember the shakiness in his voice as he uttered, "Yah, I'm sorry for that. You guys are the only family I got. You're not gonna tell anyone now are ya? Are we good now?" Yeah, I was good with that for a while. He apologized and acknowledged it. I didn't need to tell my family. That apology was all that I required.

But Amy further encouraged me to tell my family and not hang onto their secret any longer. I just couldn't. I was so ashamed. I felt old enough to know better and quite frankly, the attention of the abuse felt good. So I asked her to tell my parents. They were shocked. After they confronted my uncles, one of them said, "I would cut off my right arm if I could take it back. I'm so deeply sorry." The other uncle, who initially apologized to me on the phone, denied it publicly until his untimely death by suicide last April. It divided and divorced our family. But I know and he knew. Today, it no longer matters to me who believes it. It happened.

I spent the entire decade of the 90's so lost and disconnected from my body, my past, and my purpose. I was completely directionless. I self-sabotaged everything I did and could not maintain any kind of long-term relationship. I pickled my liver in alcohol, and lived just to have fun. I jumped from therapist to therapist, from counselors to preachers, from psychologists to psychiatrists, from EMDR therapy to personal development seminars and ropes courses. I was desperately looking for someone or something to "fix" me and make me feel better and whole and relevant.

Anti-depressants made me homicidal and suicidal. "I want to jump off my balcony right now. I want to shoot the people who did this to me and f***ed up my life," I said to the therapist while living in Hawaii. "You have to help me. Stop me. Do something. Get me off of these pills before I do something stupid. This drug is affecting my brain and making me think things I normally don't think. I'm just not me. I will not take these pills another moment longer."

That was the last time I ever took an anti-depressant or saw a therapist. I was always looking for something outside of me.

In addition, I spent two years lobbying, and finally succeeded in a crusade to increase the criminal statute of limitations for sex crimes on children in the State of Wisconsin. My grassroots effort was dubbed 'The Bogan bill'. Though its sister bill is the one that was actually enacted into law, it was still gratifying to be a part of a state-wide movement that was bigger than me and will outlive me.

I thought that working to pass the Bogan Bill was my cleansing, my clearing, and my healing. "Okay, we're done with this now. This is never going to affect me again." It simply wasn't true. I went more than two decades of my life with 'Victim' branded on my forehead. It wasn't until I embarked on reading and researching things that felt correct for me, that led me to self-healing, which ultimately led me to Sherry Anshara and the QuantumPathic® Center of Consciousness. Here I was introduced to the QuantumPathic® Energy Method (QPEM).

Out of all my therapists from Wisconsin to Hawaii, no one ever suggested the answers were within. Imagine the time, effort, money, and experience I could have saved had somebody shown me how to connect with my body and assisted me in recognizing and awakening my own inner power.

This is what carried me through: I submersed myself in personal development books and tapes and meditations. I would fall asleep listening to subliminal and motivational messages and re-loop them all night long for eight hours straight. I would listen to them while cleaning the house, showering, getting ready for work, and driving in the car. I became obsessed with inputting good and positive things into my brain, soul, and being. This led me to yoga. That led me to eating cleaner, or a little more whole. Which then led me to working out, taking care of my body, and exercising my heart. Then I was led to read deeper books and attend personal development seminars to learn about expanding my consciousness. This ultimately led me to the QuantumPathic® Energy Method (QPEM) out here in Arizona.

How did I get to Arizona? Two years ago I was sitting in my office in Wisconsin. It was a chilly October morning. I had my feet on my desk and was looking at my "Dreams Can". It's a product I created. I sell them at my motivational speaking events, workshops, and seminars. Inside of this Dreams Can I have about 700 cards on which I hand-wrote everything I desire to be, do, share, and experience in my lifetime.

Every couple of months when I feel so inclined, I reach in the Can and randomly draw something out. That day I pulled the card that said, "Go winter somewhere warm for 90 days." On the back were five choices from Arizona to Florida to Costa Rica. I closed my eyes and said, "Eeny meeny miny mo," and my finger landed on Arizona.

Fourteen days later, I got on an airplane with no business contacts, connections, or resources, hardly knowing anyone. It was a fun self-imposed challenge to see what I would and could create for my life and business.

My dream was to winter some place warm and run my speaking and coaching business from anywhere in the world with just a laptop and a cell phone. This was my sure-fire test to prove that my coaching program worked because I was living the adventure and achieving the results live in front of my social media audience. I came here with that one desire but ended up with a whole new discovery and awareness.

I now feel that my energy drew me to Arizona just to experience the QuantumPathic® Energy Method (QPEM). In such a short time, I released something I didn't consciously know was still frustrating me and holding me back from playing bigger. After all, another decade had passed and by all accounts, I was living my dream life. I had backpacked around the world, written a few books, had a winter and summer condo, vacationed 100 days a year, and was running a successful speaking and coaching business for entrepreneurs.

I had come a long way from the factory job I started off with during my turmoil and I was proud of all my achievements. The only thing missing was a loving and committed relationship, the lack of which I blamed on my busy life-on-the-move lifestyle. I was "good" and things were "good".

And then I found the QuantumPathic® Energy Method (QPEM) or it found me! I discovered a whole new set of tools, a whole new practical application for connecting with my body, and a whole new method of releasing and cleansing that I didn't even know I required, and I got clear on why my relationships weren't working and what was holding me back from really achieving my own boldest goals and most daring dreams. I didn't know what I didn't know. And then I did.

If I could press a button or take a pill and make my sexual abuse go away, as if it never happened, or make my sexuality, which I've denied my entire life, disappear, I wouldn't do it. It is a piece of who I am and I embrace the whole, bona fide me.

My intention is to pass on the lessons and knowledge as best as I can through my own experiences, and share them with you from which you can grow and be prosperous, be inspired and empowered. Whatever your demons are or whatever skeletons you are hiding in your closet, you too can move past and grow beyond them. Today is the perfect day for you to make a new choice and choose a new life or a new way.

I feel like my soul has emerged for the very first time. My soul has taken its very first breath of life with a new heartbeat into my life. After all the years I spent soul searching to find some method to bring ease, peace, and balance into my life, it was finally met when I discovered the QuantumPathic® Energy Method (QPEM), which led me to ME. I met ME, my true self and my Perfect Child Within (PCW), and they melded into one. It all arrived in perfect time.

Now that I am here, it is a beautiful feeling. I feel an inner peace and unity that I have never felt before. I am whole and perfectly expanding. I am connected with my body and my life purpose, which is leading entrepreneurs to achieve their boldest goals, most daring dreams, and live their authentic, empowered life through my professional speaking and coaching services.

Here is how I start my day:

Every morning when I wake up, I do the QuantumPathic® Energy Method (QPEM) process of connecting with my body, which I learned in the Healing at Your Core workshop. As a result, my day flows and my attitude escalates. Everything improves. My relationships with clients, family, and friends are better because I'm operating from a different frequency and vibration. I start my day and my business calls from a place of heartness and intention. I am the one who creates my day, my schedule, and my life. Life no longer runs and controls me.

First, I open up my crown chakra and lay down. I feel the energy flow to my fingers and toes. Then I connect, acknowledge, and thank my body and ask what my body requires for the day. The body knows all the answers.

If I am experiencing pain, I ask my body:

1. **What does the space or place in the pain look like?**
2. **How old am I in the space, place, or pain?**
3. **What is the root cause of the pain?**
4. **What message is the pain sharing with me?**

Then I am being the process to honor, release, and clear the pain.

I always choose to experience a release and deep connection with my body and myself. Because I connect to my body and acknowledge my body, my consciousness is coming from my heartness instead of my thinky thinky brain.

Here is one of the particular breakthroughs I had while implementing the QuantumPathic® Energy Method (QPEM) at home. I have had left hip, SI Joint, and low back pain for twenty plus years. So one morning, I chose to get to the root cause to clear this pain and discomfort. I began with my throbbing hip, cradling it with my hands and asked my body the questions I learned in the Healing at Your Core workshop.

This particular day, through my mind's eye, I noticed my five-year-old self was in a cage, like the ones they use for dogs. The cage was lying next to the right side of my body, which is the male manifesting side of the body.

Every morning for weeks, in my mind's eye, I'd walk over and coerce or drag my five-year-old self out of this cage and stand her up. Because she's been in this cage, she is like a puppet with wobbly legs. I shake her until her legs get strong enough to stand on her own. Then she stands firmly and cheerfully walks to the left side of my body. And we start our day.

I was getting so frustrated seeing my five-year-old self inside of this cage. Then one morning, I started swearing and said to the five-year-old *ME* in the cage, "I do not require you to be in this cage anymore! You get your ass out of this cage yourself. You are strong enough to get out of the cage yourself! DO IT NOW! Get your ass out here now!" Every day, my five-year-old self would get out of the cage. I'd send her to the left side, which is the female creator side of the body. Then we'd start our day.

Then I attended my second workshop, Head to the Heart. This is where I had some of the most profound breakthroughs of my entire life. The Monday after the workshop, I sat down to do my morning meditation and there was no cage!

The five-year-old child who I had connected with during the weekend workshop experience was in the shape of a starburst with her fists raised above her head in "victory" and her legs stretched out below her. She was ever so perfectly positioned in my solar plexus/heart area. Like a perfect-fitting puzzle piece facing the world with me, centered in my chest. She had a huge smile on her face. I was beaming too!

That was my Perfect Child Within (PCW). We were truly connected in this moment. It was a new feeling inside, a new layer of strength, and it was bold and beautiful. I had the greatest sense of purposefulness and love for her. This was the biggest shift I had so far in working with the QuantumPathic® Energy Method (QPEM), applying the tools I learned. A sense of purpose, a feeling of connection, and an expansion of consciousness happened.

About a week later, my five-year-old self kept showing up, just as she had in my daily meditations. I was always so happy to see her. She was still cage-less, but she was lessening and fading. Sometimes she was happy, sometimes she was sad. And then, she was just sad.

I didn't feel her power or *the* power anymore. Here was this little girl dragging her feet and bowing her head before me in our morning meditations. I was frustrated again. When I asked her what was bothering her, it always came back to her pain of being sexually abused and not being believed by some family members. Why did the same sexual abuse story keep coming up in every area of my body we chose to work on during the body scan? Why!!

"I'm sick and tired of this story," I said to Sherry Anshara during a phone call. "I don't require it anymore. I'm releasing it. I don't want to talk about it anymore and how it has affected me. I am done with it! How much frigging longer can this take? Will this abuse continue to affect, effect, and infect my life and continue to rob me of fully living?!"

Then Sherry Anshara said, "Instead of demeaning this five-year-old Traci for showing up again because she is in pain, crouch down on your knees, get face to face with her and ask her what message she has for you."

When I asked my five-year-old Perfect Child Within she said, "I require you to believe in me, to love me, to trust me, and to get out of our way. I have known what to do from the beginning. I have gotten us this far, NOT you!" She pointed a finger firmly at me, the adult. "Your adult Childish Adult Ego is standing in the way of your relationships, businesses, finances, wellness… everything, because you make a decision, then you second guess yourself and try to change courses. You are not making choices. You are making emotional decisions."

"Me, your Perfect Child Within, says to you...You don't trust in yourself or *me*. You don't believe in yourself or *me*. You are the one who does not feel worthy...and that is your issue, not mine! I know what to do. I know we are worthy. If you would get out of your own way, surrender and trust, I, your Perfect Child Within can take charge of our life from here. We meld as *all*, not *one*. We are *Allness*."

My five-year-old Perfect Child Within put me in my place. She called me on my stuff. I embraced her. It was a beautiful moment. I honored and thanked her for standing up for our truth, for not allowing me to get in the way any longer. For reminding me if I trust and surrender to the highest and greatest good of our consciousness, all will be provided and all will be perfect and all will show up in divine order.

This is what led to my five-year-old Perfect Child Within, in my solar plexus/heart area, smiling and beaming because we are now whole, we are now *Allness*. We are connected. Before, I felt her as a separate person from me. Now I know we are together and we are *Allness*. She is me. We are this strength and this divine source energy.

In the past, when I went through the QuantumPathic® Energy Method (QPEM) connecting process, the opening of the solar plexus/heart, I always experienced two sources conflicting with each other. One was anger; the other was Source energy.

I realized I liked hanging onto the anger because anger was my greatest motivator. I could be prodded and pushed to anger. Some days it's like boiling water. It only takes one degree to move from hot water to boiling water. When it reaches that one degree to boiling anger this is when I propel into action. I call it my boiling anger ball. I make things happen when we get to this temperature.

That's the space from which I created the 'Bogan Bill'. From this anger space, I backpacked around the world. Then I wrote my first book because nobody believed I could. Then I went to college at age 35 and got straight A's. Then I moved to Hawaii with $800 in my pocket with the same anger. Through this anger, I was motivated by that one degree to the boiling anger point. I realized I liked it. I wanted to hang onto it.

That last weekend at the Head to the Heart workshop, I cleared the anger to only allow that Source energy. There was nothing in my solar plexus/heart but this ball, a deep blue color that doesn't exist on Earth. It is a color that had sound, a color that had a heartbeat, a color that was alive or was life. This giant globe was churning in a slow roaring motion. It looked like the shape and size of Earth with a more piercing presence.

As it swung in a slow rotation, my five-year-old self was facing me, then my adult self, then my child self, then my adult self, slowly spinning round and round in deafening slow motion. I could hear the heartbeats of my five-year-old child and my adult self merge.

I felt alive for the very first time in my life. The giant globe went from the blue-looking Earth to this massive energy ball that was the color of Saturn. Her power and brilliance intensified before my being until I felt her in my core, and then as my core. We were Allness! Source energy! Pure love!

In this moment, I realized that my whole life I had been attempting to control the movement of this force, through my boiling anger ball, instead of surrendering to or allowing the power, this beautiful Source energy to move me. I realized with Real Eyes that I had been attempting to control and manipulate this energy instead of allowing it to move me into flow.

My Power, my Source energy vs. the force of my Childish Adult Ego is my boiling anger ball and the pain of conflict within me. This conflict and pain led me to purpose. I went from breathing to being breath. I achieved going from life's motions to living my life fully. From being angry to being love. From being a victim to being a thriver!

I've had such incredible transformation and expansion in my life since implementing the QuantumPathic® tools and the practical applications of the tools that I learned through the QuantumPathic® Energy Method (QPEM). As a result, I have referred more than 100 family, friends, and clients to the workshops and one-on-one sessions with Sherry Anshara in just nine months.

Several of my friends have gotten on airplanes from all corners of the country to experience the workshop, sight unseen, with few questions asked, just based on my 'word' that this was genuine, real, and worth it.

I wish you a happy life!
It's your time to Dream it. Plan it. Live it!
Enjoy the Adventure!

Traci Bogan, Dreampreneur

A GIFT FOR YOU!
10 Day Transformational Dare:
I am gifting you 10 days of transformational activities and worksheets that will assist you to creating your authentic empowered life! Simply text **dare** to 96000 to begin your Transformation NOW!

www.TraciBogan.com
Traci@TraciBogan.com

FROM A MEDICAL AND SCIENTIFIC PERSPECTIVE

"Your body is your intelligence…
your brain only computes limitations…
STOP THINKY-THINKING!"

-Sherryism

Many Roles, Many Methods

by Christina Kovalik, N.D.

My own QuantumPathic® journey to awareness began in an Intuitive Powers/Practical Applications 1 class Sherry Anshara offered for naturopaths. As a recent graduate from a medical naturopathic school and new mother of a six-month-old son, I had little confidence in my business. My voice was stifled. I also felt deeply disappointed by the lack of depth in my school's training of the mind/body connection. With my interest in energy medicine, I knew the importance of clearing my own stuff first before I could assist others to do so.

After the first QuantumPathic® class, I realized that I had the power to alter my thinking and learn more efficient ways to express myself by living my truth through my heart. What this means is that I could focus on my true heart's desires by releasing any limited beliefs blocking my outcome. I realized that I had acquired outdated belief systems, emotions, and traumas that were holding me back from who I desired to be.

QuantumPathic® came to me at the right time in my life. My confidence in business was low, and my voice, my expression, and my communication was stifled. From my childhood up to that point, I was often afraid to use my voice. I denied what I truly desired. I was afraid of what others would think. I worried about how my feelings might affect others. I also had concerns what others may say in response to my feelings. I was like a scared little girl. After the first class, I realized that I had the power to change my thoughts, alter my thinking, and learn more efficient ways to express myself by living my truth through my heart.

Thoughts and words are very powerful. My body was holding on to those traumas, emotions, and self-limiting thoughts that were not serving me. Waking up and becoming aware of the root emotions, traumas, and beliefs that were stored at the cellular level allowed me to release them and lighten my energetic body. My life has been forever changed. QuantumPathic® has become a breath of fresh air under my wings, guiding me through the adventure of life. It now affects my children as well.

Although, I had a very healthy pregnancy, the delivery was long and challenging. I chose a natural birth using hypnobirthing, which is the process of self-hypnosis, deep breathing, and focusing. This assisted me through the delivery process, which made it seem like it was 20 minutes instead of the 2 hours it took for the delivery.

Immediately after he was born, he had trouble breathing and had seizures shortly after birth. He was taken away from me. I didn't get to see him until the next day. He was in the NICU (neonatal intensive care unit) for three weeks. This was one of the hardest times in my life. How challenging to miss out on the natural mother-baby bonding experience!

Constantly, I worried about his health, experiencing the emotion of a great loss at not being able to hold him. To top it off, it was close to the holidays. How could I celebrate when my son wasn't with us? At last, he was allowed to come home. Then on that same day, I was admitted to the hospital for a postpartum hemorrhage which was caused by an extra placenta of a twin that didn't form.

Through the QuantumPathic® classes and my individual sessions with Sherry Anshara, I was able to release the emotional traumas and guilt associated with this experience. After releasing the trauma, I was able to realize and comprehend my son chose this path. He chose this experience. Whatever life experiences he chooses, it is his contract with himself. I also understand that this is the contract that we both agreed upon between us.

Several months later, I had an overactive thyroid. Thyroid issues are more likely to present themselves after a stressful event such as childbirth. I sought out the allopathic way to address the imbalance just to get the information. I had intentions of treating it naturally and to discover the energetic pattern of what had caused it.

As I stated earlier, I was a very shy, soft-spoken child growing up. I was afraid to speak my truth, afraid of what others may think or feel about me. I stuffed my feelings and internalized them, instead of feeling secure and confident in the importance of what I think, feel, and say is important. All of this behavior seemed to stem around relationships and public speaking. I remember being in certain relationships and afraid to speak my mind. It was a common thread that I chose to break. I did this by pushing myself to grow with personal and spiritual development and leadership courses.

I believe that certain people have lessons to work through in this life. I also believe that some people have weakened energy centers that also relate to issues they have to work through in this lifetime. I continued to find ways to push myself into situations that are out of my comfort zone. By doing that, I built up my confidence in who I am and what I have to offer my patients while continuing to work on my communication. Pushing myself to grow spiritually, personally, and professionally, I focused on ways to expand my throat chakra (energy center), by opening my internal and external communication systems and my creativity.

Around the same time, I started personal development training with Michael Bernoff, a personal development coach, to improve my communication skills, increase my confidence level and grow in different directions. The personal development coincided with the QuantumPathic® trainings in supporting me to get out of my own way and create the life that I desire to live. Building up my confidence gave me more opportunities to speak my truth, allowing my words to be powerful and expanding my throat chakra.

Five years later, my thyroid issue resurfaced when I stuffed my desire to have another child. My second son was three years old and my oldest was five. The strong desire for a third child started happening off and on. I didn't discuss this with my husband. I emotionally beat myself up about the timing, hiding my feelings, and not validating my true heart's desire. I was fearful of what he would think or say, fearful that the baby spirit that I had been sensing for so long would not come to fruition. I would hint of my desire but never clearly voiced it to my husband.

Two years later, I broke down several times crying, trying to deal with it on my own. I decided to stop beating myself up, get out of my head, and focus on expressing my heart's desire to my husband. I opened up to him in a very loving way. He considered the opportunity, but determined he was content with the two beautiful boys we are blessed to have. He stated his own fears of being an old parent, unable to financially provide for another child, and his worry about caring for our oldest son with Autism. He had trouble understanding how I could feel a sense of loss for someone who wasn't physically here.

For my own healing, I had several sessions with Sherry Anshara to release the bands of fear, to clarify the contract, and connect to the baby spirit. We also went for a couple's hypnotherapy session focused on understanding my desire and how we could work through it together. It was important for my husband to understand my desire and connection with the baby spirit who was not physically here. It was a struggle to let go of the desire I had felt so strongly for so many years. I had moments of feeling acceptance for the possibility that what I desire may not come to be. Yet the yearning for my true heart's desire rang loudly as the spirit baby knocked on my door. How could I not continue to stand in my truth?

As time passed, I now feel a great sense of peace and acceptance. My desire for a third child became a healing process as I mourned the loss of allowing the baby spirit who I felt was destined to be a part of our family. The turning point was my husband's complete understanding. With that understanding came acceptance, and I allowed myself to heal. Now, I have completely let go of the idea of having another child and I love each moment with the two boys that I do have.

This whole experience made me question my own intuitive abilities. I believe the purpose of that spirit was to promote healing in my throat center and heart. This experience has assisted my husband and me in having more open communication and love for each other on many levels.

Perhaps my own experiences with QuantumPathic® are invaluable in assisting and understanding how many infertility patients feel. Here are some examples of how I utilize the QuantumPathic® Energy Method (QPEM) tools in my practice with infertility patients and children.

**Names have been changed for patient confidentiality.*

Jack*, age 42, was struggling with a low sperm count and desired to have a child with his current wife. He had already fathered a child in a previous marriage without difficulty. However, his recent vasectomy reversal was inflamed. He was stressed out. We did weekly acupuncture sessions and I prescribed some herbs and supplements to promote his healing. I often use the QuantumPathic® Energy Method (QPEM) with my acupuncture session. The acupuncture and the energy work assist to remove the energetic blockages. This allows healing to occur. The QuantumPathic® Energy Method (QPEM) assists the flow of Qi to move more easily during an acupuncture session, making the treatment more effective.

During Jack's session, we determined that he was holding onto stress regarding his ex-wife. She was always giving him a hard time and he felt he was giving his power away to her. By bringing awareness to the solar plexus area, I used breath work and the QuantumPathic® Energy Method (QPEM) tools to assist him in releasing the dense energy from his cells. In this case, it was his ex-wife stuck in his cells. Once he released this tension and relaxed more, his body felt lighter and calmer. In time he was able to heal himself, and his sperm count and quality normalized. Six months later, he fathered a baby boy who is now 1-1/2 years old.

Becky*, age 37, desired to get pregnant. Her husband's sperm was normal. Her cycles were regular but her cycle was too long (38-40 days in between periods). She was also working 60 hours per week. We did a full blood work up and checked her hormones to discover the physical imbalances. We corrected those with herbs and supplements. We did weekly acupuncture sessions treating her adrenal glands and regulating her menstrual cycle to prepare her body energetically for pregnancy.

During one of the sessions, she realized that she had a fear of being like her mother who always seemed to push her away, as if she were a bother to her. We used the QuantumPathic® Energy Method (QPEM), my intuition, and her visualizing and feeling to identify where the blockages were. She became the NEO, the Non-Emotional Observer, stepping outside of her fear to view the root of her trauma or self-limiting belief as if watching a movie.

I am continually fascinated by the process of clearing the dense energy and watching the patient's body shift and change. Peeling away the energetic layers is like peeling an onion. The imbalances block the flow of Qi (energy) in the body's meridians or energy channels, creating disease or illness.

Once we identified and released the cellular memory of her mother in her womb chakra, Becky let go of that fear and embraced the opportunity to be the mother she desired herself to be. Once the dense energy released, I had her imprint affirmations of a healthy pregnancy and create a loving space for the baby/womb. She got pregnant three months later, and the result nine months later, she delivered a healthy baby girl.

Kara*, eight-year-old girl, presented with diffuse belly pain. She had no signs of infection, fever, or irregular bowel movements. We did a basic blood panel that was clear. I did some cupping, a Chinese treatment to release tension in her back and to open her chest. I also included acupuncture in her treatment. I held her head and initiated the QuantumPathic® Energy Method (QPEM), using my intuition and talking with the patient. She discovered that she was worried about a classmate friend, who was very sick. When I asked her where she felt it in her body, she said in her stomach. She had fears of being sick herself and anxiety. Her parents were also going through a divorce and she felt unsettled. We talked through it and released it with deep breathing and affirmations of "I am healthy, I am confident, and I am safe." I also gave her some Bach flower homeopathic remedies to help with the emotional transition. She was much better after the session and her mother said she was much calmer.

TIPS FOR PARENTS TO RAISE CONSCIOUS, HAPPY CHILDREN

1. Live Consciously and Practice Conscious Parenting

Through Sherry Anshara's teachings, I have learned the importance of this statement which became very clear to me when going through the Intuitive Powers classes. The experiences that presented during the class allowed me the opportunity to identify and release any non-serving thought patterns, emotional dramas, and limiting beliefs that were imprinted in me or in others. I gained ultra awareness of the power of words and actions on others and how it can affect me. My own thought patterns and beliefs had been influenced by the imprinting which created blockages in my own body.

As my husband went through some of the Intuitive Powers classes to better himself, he saw the importance and duty as a parent to be consciously aware of the power of our words, thoughts, and actions. What an amazing opportunity to raise our children consciously!

Let me also say that we are not perfect parents. We make mistakes and learn from them. There are times that we have to keep each other on track if a challenge with one of the kids happens and either my husband or I are off. What this means, for example, is when we have a stressful and long day, we, as parents, may not respond with the highest intentions or objectivity. We may say something that is *hurtful* or maybe we do not respond consciously.

When and if this happens, we explain what is happening to the child. We explain that he is important to us. We apologize for not being present. We explain that what he or they is expressing, feeling, or communicating is important to us. Then we can create a solution together as a family. During good and bad times, we ultimately strive to practice and live consciously. We know that what and how we say things to our children can influence and imprint in their physical and energetic bodies. This consciousness has brought huge awareness and openness in our family.

Our children are becoming more and more aware of the power of their own words and actions. And even if they don't understand at first, we proceed to give them the support required until they learn, see, and feel how it affects them. Sometimes it can take time for the kids to get it. Each child has his own individual challenges. We assist them in working through their day to day challenges knowing that we are here to support and guide them every step of the way. At the same time, we are influencing them to be conscious, independent individuals.

My oldest son is eleven and has confidence issues. We are continuously looking for ways to build up his confidence. We have enrolled him in swim lessons, gymnastics, and karate at different times in his life. Each time he advanced to the next level, he feels very accomplished. We make a big deal out of it.

Since he was eighteen months old, he has been told by speech, occupational therapists, teachers and doctors that he doesn't do things the right way. He was diagnosed with a developmental/speech delay. He would often babble with unclear words, challenged by his inability to put one or two word phrases together.

When he was six, we had a session with Sherry Anshara to see where the speech delay had stemmed from. In the session, she talked with him, held his head, and supported him to connect to his own internal flow of energy. We discovered he was speaking another language from a previous Asian life. I feel that with that awareness he was able to work through the block. After that session, his speech changed. His words became clearer and he improved greatly.

We continue to encourage building his confidence day by day in spite of his learning challenges. He was diagnosed at age six with highly functioning Autism spectrum disorder and dyslexia at age eight. We are continuing to learn ways to improve his learning process with a specialized private reading tutor that focuses on assisting my son to learn to read the way HE learns.

He has made huge strides in this area because we chose to not own the diagnoses given to our child. Instead, we are supporting him by creating the space to allow him to learn the way he was meant to learn, not the way society says he should learn. We know that he deserves to have the best opportunity to be the best that he can be. Our ultimate goal for him is to be a strong, confident, independent individual.

When he is confident, his face lights up, his eyes twinkle, he stands up tall. He speaks with confidence in things he knows and feels are his right. He still has some challenges expressing his feelings at times. When that occurs, I allow him the space if he requires space, or hugs if he requires a hug. He is such an amazing, dedicated, caring, loving, sweet-hearted boy with the biggest heart. He cares for so many, animals and people. I cherish him and am blessed he is in our lives.

Our youngest son is very strong-willed, confident, persuasive, and strong-minded. He does not like to be told how to do things and feels he is always right. He likes to do things on his own, yet gets frustrated if it doesn't work right away. He is our little gladiator. He will be a strong leader.

When I was pregnant with him, he was very active in the womb, kicking and punching. Since birth, he has always had anger, irritability issues. One minute he was irritable, and then the next he can be the sweetest little cuddler, loving, creative and curious. During one of his anger outbursts, I would often hear others say to me, "I don't know how you do it", "You have the patience of a Saint", or "I am glad he's your kid."

From ages 3-5 when he was angry, he would punch the wall, hit things, yell and scream. It seemed very disrespectful. We knew we would have to discipline him more in a way that was not permissive or harmful. We enrolled him in karate for a year. At the same time, he had trouble with chronic constipation and was very stubborn about going on the potty. I took him to see Sherry

Anshara to discover where the anger came from and to address the constipation. She held his head and talked with him. She discovered that he had brought the anger from a past life and carried it into this life. It was like he was stuck in two worlds. The constipation stemmed from a past life where he was a prisoner and was forced to hold the stool in.

We had several sessions with Sherry Anshara. His anger outbursts were happening less. We discovered he would go to the bathroom when he was ready to go. He didn't like to be told what to do. He was holding onto old beliefs from a past life. With a couple of sessions, focusing on the constipation, I understood he was having a hard time letting the past go. Physically, he still has bouts of constipation but it is less frequent. The constipation is now controlled with persistent guidance to remind him that his body requires to go. He has made some amazing progress after the few QuantumPathic® Energy Method (QPEM) sessions. We are focused on learning new ways to teach him to express himself. Now when he gets angry, he knows how to work through it. He knows he feels so much better when he doesn't hold on to the anger, the past, or whatever the issue may be.

2. Learning Effective Communication Skills

In my desire to be a conscious parent, I sought out ways to better communicate with my boys. The outdated parenting ways of yelling or spanking them when they misbehaved is not effective for these new, highly aware kids. I came across a transformational parenting program to give me guidance on how to address defiant children and to learn effective ways to communicate with them. We created house rules of no hitting and for them to have alone time if they had anger outbursts. If they did misbehave, they would have to earn back privileges by doing chores on a point system. We still use this method when my youngest acts out. He is now nine.

We do encourage our boys to express what they are feeling in a non-destructive way. We help them work through and express their feelings. If they are not able to verbalize it, we ask them questions to help them identify it. Sometimes it is not necessary to identify what they are feeling. They know that we are here to assist them and that we love and support them.

If one of my kids is having a hard time, a bad day, or not feeling well, I do some energy work on them using some of the techniques I acquired from the Intuitive Powers/Practical Applications classes and through my own naturopathic practice.

3. Body Awareness/Open Communication with Spiritual Development

As a naturopathic doctor, this is an area that is of great importance to me. I personally feel more connected to my intuitive higher self by paying attention to my body and nurturing my mind, body and soul. I stress the importance of eating well, doing yoga/exercise, meditation, and connecting with spirit through nature and body awareness. I can't tell you how many patients are so disconnected from their bodies. They are unaware of the root emotional traumas and limiting beliefs that cause their dis-ease. Most illness and disease stems from an emotional/energetic imbalance.

I teach my patients and my children the importance of being self-aware of their physical, mental, emotional, and spiritual body, which is one and the same. With my children, we discuss body awareness and encourage them to express how their physical, mental, and emotional body feels. We are still working on these principles as our kids are growing up. I have found that by asking the correct questions, it allows the kids to be better at connecting to the way their body feels, by learning ways to express themselves, and then taking the correct action steps if necessary to feel better. I often ask them how they are really feeling on a daily basis.

I also believe that open spiritual communication is essential as well. As my boys are getting older, I feel it is my duty as a parent to bring awareness of the different religions and spiritual connection with nature, the earth and the universe. By exposing them to different ways of thinking, I am honoring their right to choose for themselves what religion, beliefs, and spiritual development will feed their souls.

My husband and I were both raised Catholic. I went to a Christian grade school as well. I was forced to attend church every Sunday until I was a teenager. My parents would drop me and my brother off for service. There were times I would sneak outside in nature for an hour instead of listening to the traditional church beliefs. I knew then that it did not serve me to sit inside. Although, I appreciate all the values that were instilled by my parents and the Catholic teachings, we choose to not practice.

In college, I felt very drawn to angels. I read books, got cards and practiced talking to them. I consider myself spiritual. I often have discussions with my children about crystals, energy, angels, spirit guides, past lives, the power of your words, listening to your intuition/gut/inner knowing and following your heart to get what you desire in life. When we have these types of discussions, I am always fascinated by the examples that the kids come up with.

We had a discussion the other day about protection and asking their guardian angel for help if they feel scared. We also discussed different types of energy and how they could use it in a positive way. I had them visualize an energetic bubble of protection around them by asking them what color it would be. I would explain to them the bubble would protect them and they can put it up anytime they feel they require it. The idea is when they felt negative/bad energy around them, the bubble would make the negative energy bounce off them, be released into the universe and not go inside them. They could ask the angels for assistance. They could also use positive affirmations daily.

We often meditate together. I put the meditation music on, dim the lights and have the boys sit with me. I encourage them to close their eyes, listen to the music and focus on their breathing. If they feel like getting up before I am done, they leave the room quietly. I also play this music at night to help them have a more restful sleep.

If my children question me about anything spiritual, I answer them as honestly as I can. I know that I don't know all the answers and am still growing and developing my own spiritual connection. It has been challenged at different times in my life and I always come back to the fact that there is a higher power. I trust my own instincts, following my inner guidance and higher power. Knowing what my heart desires and focusing my attention on what steps are required to reach my outcome is motivating. If I question what my heart desires, I meditate and ask for it to surface. My purpose is trusting my own true heart's desires and supporting others on finding their own healing path.

4. Create Good Cellular Memory

One of the most important QuantumPathic® teachings is awareness of cellular memory and how it is stored at the cellular level. I make a special point to create great childhood memories that are imprinted in my children. There are many ways to create good cellular memories, like have a family game night, invite the kids' friends and their parents over, take a craft class with your child or children, and/or plan a trip away.

For example, my husband and I make vacationing a priority. It is important to take breaks from the day to day routine of work and school and spend quality time together. Whether it is for a week, a weekend short getaway, or a day trip, the quality time spent together doing outdoor activities in nature is priceless. We wish to create lasting, fun, family memories. We often travel every two months to the beaches in Mexico, or camping in Northern Arizona or California, or road trips to National Monuments.

As the kids get older, we strive to go to at least one new place per year and know that there is a short time window to enjoy the kids at their current ages. It teaches the kids about being more present in the moment, family values, exploring new cultures/cities and exposure to the world. The vacation also allows us to rejuvenate, to practice present moment awareness, and to be better able to deal with stress.

I understand that life happens and we can't always control all the bad things that happen in life. We can control how we choose to respond to stress and the challenges in life by being consciously aware of the outside and internal influences that affect us at the cellular level. It is essential to let go of the things that don't serve us and to teach our children how to do the same.

The body is so fascinating. We all have the ability to create the life that we desire to live, and to break through old patterns or beliefs that no longer serve the higher good for oneself. It is so important to first recognize what it is that is blocking the body's innate ability to heal itself naturally. Remove the blockage, lighten up the energetic body, and then imprint newness by creating the life you desire. It is key to identify the action steps, and watch as your conscious creation unfolds.

I create a ripple effect by educating my patients, family, and friends while continuing to develop my own abilities. The ripple affects all I come in contact with. Sharing love, lightness and trusting the heart center/intuition and what makes you happy in this life is essential. I am so grateful and feel blessed to be able to share my gifts and talents with all who cross my path. Thank you, Sherry Anshara, for developing the QuantumPathic® Energy Method (QPEM)! It truly has changed my life and is a key element in my practice.

Christina Kovalik
Naturopathic Physician and Acupuncturist
drchristinakovalik.com

Transformational Bridge to Consciousness

by John Gangemi, Chiropractic Physician

The QuantumPathic® Energy Method (QPEM) is truly remarkable. Thanks to this method of getting to the core of the issue, I am transformed.

For the past two years, I have had the opportunity to attend numerous QuantumPathic® courses, as well as experience the QPEM first hand through my numerous private sessions with Sherry Anshara, the developer of the QuantumPathic® Energy Method. I have also witnessed many course participants' lives transformed as a result of the QPEM.

To begin with, I will share the feelings and experiences I have had with the QuantumPathic® Energy Method. Secondly, I will present some of the science, concepts, and developments of mind-body medicine as it relates to the QPEM. And lastly, I will offer my perspective as a chiropractic physician to other healthcare professionals who desire to expand their skills of evaluating and assisting their patients in a more holistic manner.

The title, *The Intelligence Code*, is perfect as it refers to the "innate intelligence" that is intrinsic in all human beings. The QuantumPathic® Energy Method gives us a set of tools and practical applications which, when applied, can be used to bring awareness to develop our "innate intelligence" and create the life we desire.

My Personal Transformation

The QuantumPathic® Energy Method has assisted me to become a better person, a better doctor and a better friend to my Self and others. What I've learned from QPEM is that anything unresolved in the past is unresolved now.

A perfect example of this occurred when I developed a sprain injury while running. I could hardly walk home as the pain was excruciating. Sherry Anshara correlated the seizing up of my right calf muscle with a dysfunctional Belief System and an emotional component of which I was totally unaware.

The "cellular memorization" of a past event was still unresolved and playing out in the present, manifesting as pain in my calf muscle. This was preventing me from moving forward in my life, literally and professionally.

The emotional component of this event was fear. I was in fear, not knowing which direction to take at this particular time in my life, and my body was telling me it did not like this indecision. Sherry Anshara pointed out I was sabotaging my "perfect child within", who manifests beauty, harmony and abundance in my life.

Unconsciously, I was running a dysfunctional Belief System program of "lack" that was saying, "I am not worthy of being abundant in all aspects of my life." I literally stopped my Self in my tracks from going forward. The right side of the body is the male manifesting side and the seizing of the calf represented the fear of moving forward. The dysfunctional Belief System of "lack" created fear that kept me disconnected from my inner truth, which is unlimited abundance.

The resonance of this painful experience occurred in childhood and was still playing out by creating a separation in my mind-body connection, which prevented me from stepping into my power and manifesting the life I desire.

Sherry Anshara guided me to connect with my psychosomatic network, or as she calls it, the "cellular memorization of the emotionality", to the root cause that was stored physically in my body. By guiding and focusing my awareness on this injury, it brought me back to another trauma that had occurred many years ago. I was able to connect with the emotionality and the dysfunctional Belief System of the past event and release it on a physical, mental and spiritual level. I was totally amazed that I could walk with no pain after the 90 minute session.

Being a chiropractic physician, I was very impressed to see that my posture also improved during the session. By clearing the cellular memorization, my feet, hips and spine actually realigned. Sherry Anshara pointed out to me that my forward head carriage was not genetic or a coincidence but was indicative of how hard I was pushing against life with my "computer brain". She also pointed out that my forward head posture created rounding of the shoulders, which closes off the Heart chakra connection. The Heart chakra is the highest vibrational field in the body and, when it is open, it connects you with Truth, Self and your unlimited potential. When it is closed, you are separated from your power to manifest and create health in your body and a life of beauty, harmony and inner peace.

I now comprehend that the most important relationship is with my Self! By connecting with my feelings, I am guided to a greater awareness and connection with my Self and in all my relationships. My relationships with my wife, my patients, my friends, my horse and everyone I interact with have improved on all levels. My skills as a doctor have improved. Since I have been involved with QPEM, I am more aware, present, intuitive and compassionate with my Self and with all my patients. I am so enjoying my life and my practice!

One of the principles taught at the QuantumPathic® Center of Consciousness is that when you are expressing the "real you", your energy field expands to connect with the highest vibration there is, Love. Sherry Anshara calls it "Heartness", the pure essence of the Heart. To flow with "Heartness" requires us to be vulnerable, trusting and aware; the total opposite of fearfulness.

Particle physicists have recently discovered the "Higgs boson particle", also referred to as the "God Particle". This tiny subatomic particle is associated with the transformation of energy into physical mass. Michio Kaku, theoretical physicist, professor and author, correlated this particle with the "Big Bang" Theory of the creation of the universe.

Sherry Anshara refers to the God particle as the "Akyra Zynanda particle", the divine feminine principle, the energy that creates

Life. Each individual carries within him or her this powerful energy that is waiting to be released and manifested into physical form. The Akyra Zynanda particle is activated through the resonance of "Heartness". Unconditional Love is the power that creates the universe.

Love is the power that creates everything and it is the only power that makes Life work. Since I have been applying the QPEM principles, I am learning and choosing to Love my Self fully. I have let go of the past to live in the moment where Life is thriving. I realize that you cannot Love another until you Love your Self. If you bend this universal power of Love in any way, shape or form because of the fear, you create suffering. The suffering is not to punish; it is Life's way of getting our attention to guide us back to the true "Awesomeness of our Being".

It is my feeling that every person has a responsibility to express this energy. When it is held back and not expressed, stagnation and dis-ease develop. Sherry Anshara states that health is a matter of expressing your Self fully, speaking your truth and living in the moment, free from the past.

The healing of the world or our own healing does not have to take a long time. Healing can occur at light speed when we fully embrace the consciousness of Love. Life's energy can only flow through an open Heart. Life flows to more Life, not to lack. This is where our thoughts, feelings and behaviors either are aligned with Life or not.

There is not one illness or disease in the world that cannot be healed. It's a matter of allowing your Self to choose the consciousness to Love fully. Do you Love, honor and have gratitude for your Life and for all Life? Do you trust your Self and Life completely? Are you conscious and aware? Do you feel your abundance fully? Are your dreams and desires greater than your past memories? Who is in the driver seat? Is it the emotionality of the computer brain, what Sherry Anshara calls the "childish adult ego" which has not grown up in the adult body, or is it the "perfect child within" that knows the way of the Heart?

The real rub is that, for so many, the "childish adult ego" has been running some part of our lives and is fearful of giving up control. The longer the "childish adult ego" has been in control, the more the momentum has built up. This has created a greater disconnection from Self and will take a greater effort and desire to make the shift to "Heartness". The QuantumPathic® Energy Method teaches us the practical tools and applications to detach from the control of the "childish adult ego" and reestablish the connection of "Heartness."

As Sherry Anshara states in her QPEM courses, "You create your Life moment by moment; you cannot not create! You created your pain, illness or disease and you are the only one that can change it! Change your Consciousness, change your Life on physical, emotional, mental, spiritual and financial levels; they are all the same because they are representations of how you are interacting with your Self and therefore Life."

What I find impressive are the video testimonials on the QuantumPathic® Center of Consciousness website, quantumpathic.com, which describe life-changing experiences. The testimonials from medical doctors, professionals, and lay people all document their profound life-altering experiences. Some participants documented reaching the "root cause" of their particular issue(s), allowing them to release emotional roadblocks which had prevented them from productively moving forward in their lives. Participants have shared that even after years and years of psychological therapies, various other healing modalities, and even alternative medicine therapies, they were unable to achieve effective and productive resolutions until they experienced the QuantumPathic® Energy Method.

A leader in his field of functional medicine, Anup Kanodia, MD/MPH, has stated, "The workshops are unique because not only can you get to the root cause quickly but long standing issues can often be resolved when other modalities have failed." Dr. Kanodia, a collaborator with Sherry Anshara, has referred over 500 of his patients to her. His patients have achieved outstanding healing results, emotionally, mentally, physically, spiritually, and even financially. Dr. Kanodia has connected QPEM with the field of "Psychoneuroimmunology".

Mind-Body Medicine and the QuantumPathic® Energy Method

As a chiropractic physician and a student of mind-body medicine, I always look to achieve "root cause" resolution for my patients as well as documenting the scientific mechanisms that stimulate the patient to improve. I ask my Self, "How does the QuantumPathic® Energy Method work and is there any type of scientific evidence to validate and support this method?" Quantum physics and mind-body medicine, also known as Psychoneuroimmunology (PNI), embrace the scientific principles behind the QuantumPathic® Energy Method.

Throughout my career as a chiropractic physician, I have witnessed many types of therapies and healing techniques. When you give the body what it requires, the body heals itself. The power that made the body will heal the body if you allow the body's "natural healing mechanism" to thrive.

Quantum physics today tells us that everything is energy. Although we cannot see them, our thoughts, feelings and emotions are in fact very real and have a direct impact on our health and quality of life. They trigger various chemical reactions, which can change our physiology and health for better or worse. Unresolved Belief Systems and emotions change the frequency and vibration of the body, making it difficult to access the body's natural healing mechanism for health. All healing is Self-healing and by changing your thoughts, feelings, behaviors and intentions, you are changing your body's "energetic resonance" and future probability for health, joy, and better quality of life.

"The Mind-Body Connection", a term used in holistic health professions, refers to the principle that thoughts, feelings, emotions and the body are intrinsically linked and not separate from each other. You cannot affect one of these components of health without affecting all of them simultaneously. The mind-body connection is an ancient principle in the East and is practiced in the art of Chinese and Ayurvedic Medicine. The mind-body connection was recognized in the West by the Greek physician Hippocrates. Hippocrates is considered to be the most outstanding figure in the history of medicine and is also thought to be the father of Western Medicine.

The breakdown of the mind-body connection really started with Rene Descartes (1596-1650) when he introduced the "Mind-Body Dualism Hypothesis". This impacted Western medicine for over two centuries by insisting that the mind and emotions are separate from the body. It was considered unscientific and heretical in this time period to believe the mind and emotions could ever have an impact on health. In 1964, psychiatrist Dr. George Solomon noticed that people with rheumatoid arthritis got worse when they were depressed. He began to investigate the impact emotions had on inflammation and the immune system in general. This new field came to be called "psychoimmunology".

In 1975, psychologist Dr. Robert Ader coined the term "psychoneuroimmunology" (PNI), a field he helped to create when he demonstrated that the nervous system can affect our immune system. Until then, they were considered to be unrelated. Dr. Robert Ader and Dr. Nicholas Cohen, an immunologist, conducted research experiments at the University of Rochester Medical Center, which led them to discover that the mind can affect the immune system. There is a link between what we think, our state of mind, our health and our ability to heal our Selves. It is possible for a state of mind or an emotional state to affect the immune system, the very system that is responsible for keeping the human body healthy.

Psychoneuroimmunology (PNI) became the accepted term in the scientific community of this new and exciting field of science. The more popular name soon became "mind-body medicine". PNI is an important and relatively new field that lends solid research to our understanding of the mind-body connection. In a nutshell, PNI studies the connections between behaviors, psychological processes, nervous system functions and the immune system of the body. Dr. Ader's theories that the human mind could significantly affect the ability of the immune system to fight disease were initially greeted with heated skepticism and sometimes scorn when he first proposed them more than 30 years ago. Now these principles are applied and studied in many medical specialties and scientific research centers worldwide.

Early in the 1980's, Dr. Candace Pert, a research professor in the Department of Physiology and Biophysics at Georgetown Medical Center in Washington, gave the field of psychoneuroimmunology and mind-body medicine what it lacked…a clear scientific mechanism and language which would validate further the mind-body connection. In Dr. Pert's book, *Molecules of Emotion*, she identified that the biochemicals which create emotions on the cellular level of the body are called "neuropeptides". When the neuropeptides attach to receptors located on the surface of the cell, it sets off a cascade of reactions within the cells which can have a positive or negative impact on health. She also discovered that the neuropeptides in the brain are present throughout the entire body. The brain and body are connected through a "psychosomatic" network of neuropeptides which are responsible for our awareness, emotions, beliefs, and how we experience the world.

We are currently seeing the reemergence of the mind-body connection principles in Western medicine with the implementation of programs and research at prestigious medical universities, governmental agencies, and the private sector. The National Institute of Health (NIH) has created a branch called The National Center for Complementary and Alternative Medicine (NCCAM), which studies mind-body medicine. The NIH has stated that thoughts, emotions and behaviors actually do have an impact on a person's health. This statement is impactful as it validates the importance of the mind-body connection, promoting a much more holistic approach to Western medicine. It also supports a departure from Rene Descartes' mind-body dualism hypothesis, which simply is not true.

Harvard University Medical School has been studying the "placebo phenomenon" with very favorable results. Patients' intentions and expectations can influence whether or not they get well. They call it a phenomenon but it's really mind-body medicine in action! A person's thoughts, feelings, intentions and expectations about a particular treatment can directly influence the outcome. Researchers have found that in cases involving pain, depression, anxiety, fatigue, and even some symptoms of Parkinson's, placebos can stimulate real physiological responses, such as changes in heart rate and blood pressure and changes in chemical activity in the brain.

Experimental research conducted in fields of physics and quantum physics are proving that the power of human intention affects physical reality. William A. Tiller, Ph.D., physicist, author and former professor at Stanford University, has developed the Institute for Psychoenergetic Science, dedicated to conducting research and experiments which demonstrate that the power of intention can actually affect physical reality. His experiments have used the power of intention to influence and alter the outcome of various experiments across the globe. Dr. Tiller has also used the power of intention to create outstanding results with autistic children and their families.

"For the last four hundred years, an unstated assumption of science is that human intention cannot affect what we call "physical reality". Our experimental research of the past decade shows that, for today's world and under the right conditions, this assumption is no longer correct. We humans are much more than we think we are, and the Psychoenergetic Science Institute continues to expand the proof of it." - Dr. William Tiller, Ph.D

Psychoneuroimmunology is the scientific foundation of mind-body medicine. In my opinion, the QuantumPathic® Energy Method is a bridge into the mind-body connection or the mind-body healing mechanism. Applying QPEM and observing the life changes of the participants is validating and furthering the science of PNI and mind-body medicine. It is mind-body medicine in action! The QuantumPathic® Energy Method is the common sense practical everyday application of psychoneuroimmunology/mind-body medicine that can work in the real world. As Sherry Anshara says, "The doctors and the scientists call the QuantumPathic® Energy Method an application of psychoneuroimmunology, mind-body medicine or epigenetics, but the label is really not important…only that the individual gets well."

Unresolved mental and emotional issues trigger the limbic portion of your brain to release hormones and other molecules of emotions. Your nervous system eventually gets caught up in an insidious cycle of stress which directly impacts your health. Medical researchers at the Mayo Clinic have stated, "When the nervous system is out of balance and producing an excess of stress hormones, it can disrupt almost all the body's processes, weaken the immune system and the body's ability to heal." This increases the risk of numerous health problems such as anxiety, depression, digestive problems, headaches, heart disease, sleep problems, weight gain, and memory and concentration impairment. That's why it's so important to be clear of thoughts, emotions and behavior patterns that do not serve you.

The QuantumPathic® Energy Method releases dysfunctional energetic patterns that become physical restrictions in the cell tissue via the molecules of emotions. When life energy is blocked within an individual, the natural expression of their true Self shuts down as the emotions of the "computer brain" dominate.

One of the important factors of the QPEM is that it addresses the differences between emotions and feelings. Emotions are generated by the "computer-brain", or by a term Sherry Anshara coined called the "childish adult ego". The emotions are where the troubles begin. The emotions and the emotional upsets from the past are the foundation of disease, illness, and the disconnection of the body and mind. QPEM teaches, "Feelings come from the Heart; emotions come from the computer/brain. The question is…How would you like your computer, laptop, or tablet running your life? When you live through your computer/brain, how is that working for you? When you live and create through your Heart, you are creating the best life for your Self! When you create from your computer/brain, chaos reigns."

Dr. Eric Kandel of Columbia University's Department of Physicians and Surgeons has proven that memory occurs at the cellular level at the receptor sites. Memories are not just stored in the brain, but in a "psychosomatic network" throughout the entire body. When an individual experiences a trauma, the memory of that event is stored at the cellular level within the "psychosomatic network". What is also fascinating is that Dr. Pert talks about accessing the psychosomatic network by entering into the mind-body conversation. Dysfunctional patterns of behavior can be redirected. This changes the molecules of emotions on a cellular level and alters the body's physiology for new behaviors, more feeling and greater health.

"By learning to bring your awareness to past experiences and conditions, memories stored in the very receptor of your cells, you can release your Self from these blocks, this "stuck-ness." But if the blockages are very long lasting you may need help in achieving such awareness." - Dr. Candace Pert

Dr. Pert also recommends finding health professionals that use touch therapies with counseling and guidance to assist the patient in redirecting the mind-body conversation to release their dysfunctional patterns. In my opinion, this is describing exactly what QPEM is, how it is applied and what it accomplishes. This is QPEM in a nutshell!

From a Health Professional's Perspective

The QuantumPathic® Energy Method system of body analysis and evaluation has improved my understanding of the human body from a much more holistic perspective. Being a chiropractor, I am very familiar with posture and tissue restriction when conducting a physical examination. The QuantumPathic® Energy Method of analyzing and evaluating the body has brought my understanding of the human body to a whole new level. The analysis takes into consideration not only tissue restrictions and symptomatology, but also includes the emotionality and dysfunctional Belief Systems associated with a particular dysfunctional area. The QPEM assessment and analysis is a very comprehensive holistic view of a patient. The analysis considers all aspects of a patient's health, the physical, emotional and mental components that are all interwoven in a fabric that creates health or dis-ease. Health professionals could improve their assessment, evaluation and comprehension of their patients by implementing the QPEM assessment tools.

What I have learned by observing and experiencing the QuantumPathic® Energy Method over the last two years is that health and consciousness and awareness are interconnected. If a person is stuck in the past, whether they are aware of it or not, the psychosomatic network of the mind-body is creating emotionality. This limits the functioning of the body's physiology, reduces awareness, and creates dis-ease. This can be observed when palpating an area of the body that is restricted, has developed adhesions, postural dysfunctions, and various symptomatologies. This restriction of the body's tissues will reduce the flow of energy, blood, and nerve signals resulting in dis-ease, eventually producing symptoms, and if not corrected, can produce a serious illness. Illness is not created at the time of diagnosis; it is created when your emotionality began.

Everything is connected in the mind-body. There is no separation, so when you have a feeling, an emotion or an experience, your entire being is experiencing it and recording this experience in your cellular memory. The body is the mind and the mind is the body; they are not separate. Sherry Anshara states, "You don't have to waste your time, your efforts, your creative abilities, and your life by living in the emotional connections of the past of guilt, shame, blame, regret, etc. When you do this, you make your Self sick because you are not interacting with life in the moment."

From a quantum physics point of view, you could say that health can be defined by the quality of resonance or frequency and vibration of the cell tissue. The desired resonance of health is "present time consciousness". By applying the QPEM techniques you can identify and correct dysfunctional Belief Systems and emotions which have negatively impacted your health and quality of life. You can change your resonance to live in the moment and flow from the Heart to create a life you require, desire, and deserve!

What is truly amazing is that the QuantumPathic® Energy Method puts you in the driver's seat to influence your health, your quality of life, and your abundance by what you tell your Self and through the choices you make through your Heart and your feelings. Where you place your focus is where you are literally creating your Life and your health, moment by moment. Is your focus coming from your Heart or your computer/brain? Instantly, you will know the difference.

It is my professional perspective that the QuantumPathic® Energy Method is a gateway to accessing the body's natural healing mechanism. Another way to describe QPEM is a "transformational bridge" to consciousness that leads to greater awareness of Self and better health. QPEM is based in the science of mind-body medicine. QPEM has practical applications that can be applied to all age groups from children to the elderly. QPEM assessments offer a new perspective for doctors or practitioners in the health and wellness arts who are interested in improving their comprehension and interconnectedness of the human body.

"Clear your emotional past and you clear your future."

-Sherryism

John Gangemi
Chiropractic Physician
www.healthsolutionscenteraz.com

Bibliography

Anshara, Sherry, *The Age of Inheritance: The Activation of the 13 Chakras*. Scottsdale: QuantumPathic Press®, 2003.

Anshara, Sherry, *And The Point Is…? Beyond Duality*. Scottsdale: QuantumPathic Press®, 2007.

Cherry, Kendra, "Placebo Effect Experiments, Studies, and Causes." www.verywell.com/what-is-the-placebo-effect-2795466, retrieved on September 17, 2016.

Crivii, Carmen, MD PhD, American psychosomatic society website slide show on the introduction to psychoneuro-immunology history. www.psychosomatic.org, retrieved on September 17, 2016.

Feinberg, Cara, "The Placebo Phenomenon." January-February 2013. harvardmagazine.com/2013/01/the-placebo-phenomenon, retrieved on September 17, 2016.

Kaku, Michio, "What Put the Bang in the Big Bang?" 2012, www.youtube.com/watch?v=gCnvuKb0T7E, retrieved on September 17, 2016.

Kanodia, Anup, MD., website is kanodiamd.com.

Mayo Clinic Staff, "Chronic stress puts your health at risk." April 21, 2016. www.mayoclinic.org/healthy-lifestyle/stress-management/in-depth/stress/art-20046037?pg=1, retrieved on September 17, 2016.

McGhee, Paul E., PhD., "Emotion: The Key to the Mind's Influence on Health." www.LaughterRemedy.com, retrieved on September 17, 2016.

National Institute of Health, "mind-body medicine practices in complementary and alternative medicine." www.nih.gov, retrieved on September 17, 2016.

Pert, Candace B. *Molecules of Emotion: The Science Behind Mind-Body Medicine.* New York: Scribner, 1997. 18, 143, 176, 289.

The Research of Candace Pert webpage. "Your Body is Your Subconscious Mind: Mind-Body Medicine Becomes the Science of Psychoneuroimmunology (PNI)." www.healingcancer.info/ebook /candace-pert, retrieved on September 17, 2016.

Pert, Candace B. *Your Body Is Your Subconscious Mind.* Sounds True, 2004.

QuantumPathic® Center of Consciousness seminars and course notes. www.quantumpathic.com.

Rense, Jeff, "How the Power of Intention Alters Matter with Dr. William A. Tiller." www.spiritofmaat.com/archive/mar2 /tiller.htm, retrieved on September 17, 2016.

Scott, Elizabeth, MS, "Facts about PNI and Stress." Updated September 14, 2016. www.verywell.com/psychoneuroimmunology-and-stress-3145127.

Tiller, William A., Ph.D., Institute for Psychoenergetic Science website: www.tillerinstitute.com.

Tiller, William A. and Suzy Miller, "A new science for healing autism Prof. William Tiller & Suzy Miller VLB May 2013." www.youtube.com/watch?v=6kLP92dSoIM, retrieved on September 17, 2016.

The University of Maryland Medical Center. "Mind-body medicine." 2011. umm.edu/health/medical/altmed/treatment /mindbody-medicine, retrieved on September 17, 2016.

University of Rochester Medical Center. "Robert Ader, Founder of Psychoneuroimmunology, Dies." December 20, 2011. www.urmc.rochester.edu/news/story/3370/robert-ader-founder-of-psychoneuroimmunology-dies.aspx, retrieved on September 17, 2016.

Wikipedia, "Hippocrates." en.wikipedia.org/wiki/Hippocrates, retrieved on September 17, 2016.

The Quantum Body Remembers

by Sue Barnes, MSHCA, MSN, RN

Openness is more fruitful than seclusion in dogma.

-Kirkus Reviews

Join me on a journey and shift the current paradigm of your physical and mental state of health, your relationships, and financial status. Has your body been trying to get your attention by exhibiting signs and symptoms of fibromyalgia or depression, or is your financial state all about lack? Are you addicted to drugs or alcohol?

If you are really ready to change, you have to take charge of your life and your emotions. You have to listen to your body, not your "computer" brain. You have to get rid of your current belief systems. It is your choice and your choice alone.

QUESTIONS...to ask yourself

Whatever biological age you are, you have your parents' belief systems and even society's definitions of what you should be or do. You may also have even been swept up in the latest and greatest social media trends and peer pressure so that you can "belong". As Dr. Phil would say, "How is that working for you?" If you have self-esteem issues, and we all seem to have "issues", have you been advised to look into the mirror and say "I love myself?" Do you say affirmations, journal, or participate in group therapy with others who have "your problem" where you rehash it over and over and over again? How many prescription drugs are you on? This is the fastest and most popular "fix" in the traditional healthcare setting. Do you feel better? What are the side effects of these drugs? Are you self-medicating?

Now is the time to evaluate the methods that you are using to solve your "issues" and consider a new approach that works at the core of the emotional cause of your imbalance. What if you started listening to your body and got out of your "thinky thinky" computer brain? Neither right brain nor left brain work effectively enough to make the changes to improve your life. You get in a "create and recreate" mode if you rely on your "computer" brain. Why do you have a gut feeling or a particular disease, an ache or pain in a particular part of your body? This is where the "real brain" resides, in your body.

We have been taught to be so entrenched in a specific medical model and to take drugs, whether legal or illegal, to "fix it". Are you ready to give up your crutch or excuse for not being "all you can be"? Your body is your intelligence. However, many of us are so disconnected from our body from years and even lifetimes of trauma dramas. Actually, this is the way of Duality that I have learned at the QuantumPathic® Center of Consciousness.

So how is your body talking to you? Have you heard about cellular memory? What is it and how does it work? Is it real and can it be proven? If you want a scientific study with all the complex theories, I invite you to go to the library and look it up and make a choice based on your findings. This book, *The Intelligence Code*, is intended to provide possibilities to assist you in creating a new you so that you can understand how to implement change right here, right now!

So what is cellular memory and how does it work? What are the implications? Cellular memory is the sum total of all your experiences. The opening statement of *The Intelligence Code* states, "The minute the sperm hits the egg you are in." Cellular memory for this lifetime begins. The idea that your body knows before your mind knows is the core of the common expression "get out of your head and get into your heart".

When similar events occur or when recalling an event that is "buried" within a person's subconscious mind, the reaction can manifest as discomfort, pain, or other sensations in a particular part of the body. The concept of cellular memory, which is also referred to as body memory in alternative medicine, is both a fascinating and complex subject.

At the QuantumPathic® Center of Consciousness, several concepts are taught as the basis of the emotionality of cellular memory.

The first is the string theory as explained by the co-creator of the string field theory, Michio Kaku, Professor of Theoretical Physics, City College of New York. "If one had a super-microscope and could peer directly into an electron, one would find not a point particle at all but a vibrating string. When the super string vibrates in a different mode or note, it changes into a different subatomic particle."

At the QuantumPathic® Center of Consciousness, these strings are also identified as bands. These bands, though considered invisible, connect energetically through frequency and vibration to each other through resonance. What does this mean? These bands are the connectors to each other. If you are a victim, you send out bands with a resonance of victimhood, then an individual or group of people who resonate to the frequency and vibration of being a victimizer connect to you as the victim through the bands. And the trauma dramas begin.

The effect of frequency and vibration was best visually illustrated by Dr. Masaru Emoto, an internationally renowned Japanese scientist who used high-speed photography to document that crystals are formed in frozen water differently when specific thoughts are directed toward them. In his book, *The Hidden Messages in Water*, he found that "water has the ability to copy and memorize information". He found that the energy of human consciousness and words had a profound effect on changing ice crystals.

Throughout his book are stunning pictures of the impact of using positive words in several different languages such as *thank you, love,* or *wisdom* which formed beautiful crystals. On the other hand, words such as *kill, hate,* or *you fool* did not form a crystal or formed a dark ugly lump. A variety of music and songs were also studied, and in keeping with the energy of words, the frequency and vibration of the music or song was consistent in forming beautiful ice crystals versus those that were malformed as demonstrated by

The Beatles song "Yesterday" compared to Elvis Presley's "Heartbreak Hotel". It is a fascinating subject with phenomenal research results.

Chemical reactions associated with cellular memory can change once repressed emotions are acknowledged. According to the research by Candace Pert, Ph.D., who was a neuroscientist/pharmacologist at Georgetown University, in her book, *Molecules of Emotion*, we know that "memories are stored not only in the brain, but in a psychosomatic network extending into the body, particularly in the ubiquitous receptors between nerves and bundles of cell bodies called ganglia, which are distributed not just in and near the spinal cord, but all the way out along pathways to internal organs and the very surface of our skin."

Dr. Pert further states: "The mind and body communicate with each other through chemicals known as peptides. These peptides are found in the brain as well as in the stomach, in muscles and in all of our major organs. I believe that memory can be accessed anywhere in the peptide/receptor network."

When trauma occurs, the brain releases neurotransmitters that transmit information to the organs and musculoskeletal system via "fight or flight". This electrochemical reaction leaves a mark in the body's cellular tissue, identified as cellular memory. In subsequent events that are similar, the same reaction will re-occur based upon the subjective nature and intensity of the perceived threat. Again, this is defined as the "fight or flight" unnaturalness of Duality.

Dr. Thomas R. McClaskey, based on the concept that all memory is encoded at the cellular level, notes that in "conditions such as Post Traumatic Stress Disorder, the 'problem' is an expression of traumatically encoded information at the cellular level. In order for therapy to have lasting effect, it is imperative that a primary focus of intervention involves isolation and decoding of the causative traumatic cellular memory pattern."

Researchers have found that the heart communicates information to the brain and throughout the body via electromagnetic field interactions. The heart produces the body's most powerful and most extensive rhythmic electromagnetic field. The heart's magnetic component is about 500 times stronger than the brain's magnetic field and can be detected several feet away from the body. It was proposed that the heart field acts as a carrier wave for information that provides a global synchronizing signal for the entire body (McCraty, Bradley & Tomasino, 2004). There is an electromagnetic communication system that operates just below our conscious awareness. Energetic interactions possibly contribute to the 'magnetic' attractions or repulsions that occur between individuals (McCraty, 2004).

The heart also secretes oxytocin, which is key in childbirth and lactation. However, studies show that this hormone is also involved in cognition, tolerance, adaptation, complex sexual and maternal behaviors, learning social cues and the establishment of enduring pair bonds. Concentrations of oxytocin in the heart were found to be as high as those found in the brain (Cantin & Genest, 1986).

Michael Gershon, M.D., an expert and "father" of the field of neurogastroenterology and author of the 1998 book, *The Second Brain* (HarperCollins), viewed the enteric nervous system as "the second brain". Dr. Gershon notes that while it does not have conscious thought or decision-making capabilities, it does have an impact on the mental state and plays key roles in certain disease throughout the body. The second brain consists of sheaths of neurons embedded in the walls of the intestines and contains some 100 million neurons, more than in either the spinal cord or the peripheral nervous system. It is equipped with its own reflexes and senses and can control gut behavior independently of the brain. Emeran Mayer, M.D., professor of physiology, psychiatry and bio behavioral sciences at the David Geffen School of Medicine at the University of California, Los Angeles (U.C.L.A.) found that about 90 percent of the fibers in the vagus nerve carry information from the gut to the brain and not the other way around.

Paul Pearsall, Ph.D. researched transplant patients who experienced the donor's "cellular memories." The heart processes information about the body and the outside world through an "info-energetic code", a profuse network of blood vessels and cells acting as the circulatory system and as an energy information gathering and distribution system.

Prominent medical experts have studied the cases of recipients of heart transplants who inherited donors' memories and reported changes in their tastes, their personality, and, most extraordinarily, in their emotional memories. Claire Sylvia, who was 47 years old at the time, was the first person in New England to undergo a heart-lung transplant. She was a divorced mother of one who was a former professional dancer and dying from primary pulmonary hypertension when she had a pioneering heart lung transplant at Yale-New Haven Hospital in 1988. She was given the organs of an 18-year-old boy who had been killed in a motorcycle accident near his home in Maine. After the surgery she acquired the characteristics and cravings of the donor.

According to her book, *A Change of Heart*, two reporters came to the hospital to interview her and asked what she wanted more than anything else. She replied, "I'm dying for a beer right now" and was surprised because she did not like beer. She developed a sudden liking for certain foods like Kentucky Fried Chicken, snickers bars, and green peppers.

A simple example of the practical application of cellular memory is when you were "in trouble," your parent(s) probably said your given first name, middle name, and last name in a "stern" manner to get your attention. You get a sensation in the pit of your stomach and think "uh oh, I am going to get it" – whatever "it" is. There is now an association with your formal name and authority figures and your stomach "sinks" or does a flip flop whenever it happens with the exception of formal occasions to announce who you are. You get called into the principal's office, "uh oh," your boss calls you into their office, "uh oh!" Can you relate?

A personal example for me was an auto accident I had when I was in my early twenties. It was a beautiful day in Georgia when I was driving my bright red Fiat Spider convertible through the mountains without a care in the world. Remember those "good ole days"? Suddenly I lost control of the car and was veering toward the cliff. Panicking, I over-corrected and headed towards the embankment on the other side. Again panicking, I over-corrected yet again and went barreling toward the cliff. There was a long u-shaped curve and I could see that there were no cars coming towards me on the other side of the gorge.

Rational thoughts flooded my mind: "Oh my gosh, I am going to die and no one will see me!" Then as I hurdled toward the cliff I thought, "Why am I not seeing my life flash before my eyes like it's supposed to happen!"

As my intelligent body took over, I "blacked out" with no recollection of flipping my car over the cliff, hurdling down into the ravine, nose-diving the front of the car, or even flipping over and smashing the rear bumper.

The car actually rolled over two or three times, ending right side up. What an adventure! I have no recollection or memory of me removing my seat belt. My first conscious awareness was of me standing on my seat looking at the back of the car, seeing smoke. "Oh no," I thought. "The car is going to catch on fire and will explode!" Jumping out of the car, I literally crawled up the embankment. Of course, being the brave female that I was, I thought snakes were probably in the grass, which hastened my ascent to the side of the road.

The first car that drove by did not see me. I was lying on the ground. When I was able to stand up, I flagged down the next car. The driver radioed for help and drove me to the closest medical care. My only injuries were a big black and blue mark from the seat belt which had saved my life. My body was full of aches and stiffness from the muscle trauma. Needless to say, structural changes occurred in my body, causing major whiplash issues in my neck.

How does that event apply to cellular memory? Those who have ever been in a car with me will testify to my physical reactions, especially in the mountains going around curves. They know I get very nervous when I hear the sound of squealing tires. Imagine me on the 101 highway travelling from Los Angeles to Carmel! The queasy stomach comes right after the white knuckles, the sweating begins, and the terror sets in followed by multiple requests to slow down. When I am the driver, yes, I become that "little ole lady from Pasadena".

This is irrational fear at its peak. To those who have not experienced it, they think I am a "silly goose" for freaking out as we go around the big curves on the freeway where there are overpasses and underpasses galore. To release this fear, the QuantumPathic® Energy Method takes me to those parts of my body which react irrationally to everyday travel. I have learned, through QPEM, not to relive this traumatic event. A QPEM tool that I use frees my "inner child" from fear. How do I do this? I replace the fear with conscious choices supporting myself from my heart, not my "computer" brain, to comprehend that I am safe and secure within my adult body in the current moment. Therefore, the past traumatic cellular experiences of the accident no longer have the emotional and physical impact on me or my body to make me afraid over and over again.

Now, apply this principle to your own emotional traumas that you may or may not be aware of. The unaware traumas are the ones that insidiously affect you at your cellular level by making you afraid or sick. When these situations occur and you think you don't have an answer to your emotional state or to the fears that are being generated by you, this is the opportunity to step back and connect to your cellular memory in your body. Your body will provide clear answers as long as you stay out of your emotional "computer" brain.

During these fearful moments, your body compensates or reacts to these conscious or unconscious traumas. Here is a great example of pain relating to an emotional attachment to the past. Do you have shoulder pain from always feeling responsible for everyone and everything for as long as you can remember? Shoulder pain equals unrealistic responsibility for others in your life.

Do you have throat issues from not speaking your truth? Do you sabotage yourself because you believe you are not worthy of everything life has to offer? Do you have chronic fatigue from carrying around the weight of the fear programs? Utilizing the QuantumPathic® Energy Method does not involve "reliving" the event. But by being the Non-Emotional Observer, you cut these "bands" that keeps you stuck in the past.

How do you cut the bands? By your willingness to detach from your past issues and the people stuck in your bands. You are cutting the bands to all the individuals, times, and events to which you are dysfunctionally attached. Free yourself and you may even free "them" by cutting the bands.

Remember, you have not been taught to see the bands, even though they are physical. Through the courses at the QuantumPathic® Center of Consciousness you are taught to see the bands. Because they are physical, you are physically connected to the "them", to the past experiences and to the trauma dramas that relate to the situation. As you cut the bands, you will feel lighter.

You are actually letting go of carrying the weight of the wait. What this means is the molecules of emotions are physical, snotty, gelatinous, goopy, thick, and icky. As you release these heavy, physical molecules of emotions, you do feel lighter. Perhaps this is the real description of the "light body". By letting go of all the heavy, emotional crap, you step into the moment and free yourself by cutting the bands that are not serving you.

For the relationships and experiences of the past that do serve you, don't cut the bands. Expand upon them, and create deeper, more productive, and stable relationships.

I leave you to ponder the fate of Paul William "Bear" Bryant who was the head coach for the University of Alabama football team for 25 years. He led his team to six national championships and thirteen conference championships. When he turned 69 he decided to retire after the 1982 season. After the last game of the season, he was asked what he planned to do now that he was retired. He replied, "Probably croak in a week."

Four weeks after making that comment, and just one day after passing a routine medical checkup, on January 25, 1983, Bear Bryant checked into Druid City Hospital in Tuscaloosa after experiencing chest pain. A day later, when being prepared for an electrocardiogram, he died after suffering a massive heart attack. Was coaching football his "life" and did it define him? Was his body following his wishes? You decide.

"Be clear what you say about yourself.
It may mean life or death."

-Sherryism

Bibliography

Emoto, Masaru. *The Hidden Messages in Water.* Hillsboro, OR: Beyond Words Publishing, Inc., 2004. Translated by David A. Thayne. xviii, 4, 22-23.

Kaku, Michio. *Einstein's Cosmos: How Albert Einstein's Vision Transformed Our Understanding of Space and Time; Great Discoveries.* New York: W. W. Norton & Company, 2004. 226.

McClaskey, Thomas R, D.C. *Decoding Traumatic Memory Patterns at the Cellular Level.* The American Academy of Experts in Traumatic Stress, Inc., www.aaets.org. 1998.

Pert, Candace B. *Molecules of Emotion: The Science Behind Mind-Body Medicine.* New York: Scribner, 1997. 143.

Sylvia, Claire and William Novak. *A Change of Heart - A Memoir.* 1997.

A Testimonial

by Dwight McKee, MD, CNS, ABIHM

Sherry Anshara is the most remarkable medical intuitive/healer that I have met in my life. She is the creator of a unique process that unlocks deep-seated emotional pain, stress, and trauma by facilitating the release of core issues that reside in the body. The end result for me has been a deep sense of calm and peace and freedom from some severe physical issues.

I had learned of Sherry Anshara's work from an old friend of mine, Cyndy Tercha, in the summer of 2014. At that time, I ran into her at a medical conference on the east coast. The medical professional friends I invited to form the workshop were interested both from a personal and a professional perspective, but none of us knew quite what to expect.

I organized a 2 ½ day workshop with Sherry Anshara in November 2014 with some physician and veterinarian friends of mine with hopes that I might get some help with chronic headaches that have plagued me off and on for over 40 years.

A recent bout with kidney stones involving the placement of a dilating stent required high doses of pain medications. After all the stones were removed, I found myself unable to completely stop the pain medications without serious "medication rebound" headaches. Hence, heavy-duty medications that I had used several times a week for management of my more severe headaches became daily medication for over 3 months. I was concerned that I might never successfully get off them. I have used many integrative techniques over the years to deal with headaches, including cranial-sacral osteopathy, acupuncture, homeopathy, exercise, psychotherapy, botanicals, identification of food sensitivities, correction of "leaky gut", massage, and meditation. Yet headaches became a more frequent problem as I got older. I used pain medication more frequently until, as I said, I seemed to be stuck in a "holding pattern" with opiates and butalbital, a barbiturate which potentiates the pain-relieving effect of opiates.

I had taken both medications in the morning, about 8 hours prior to the beginning of the QuantumPathic® workshop. Amazingly, that was the last dose that I had for the next 2 weeks, which was the longest medication-free period I can remember in recent years.

In the last two months, I have taken headache medication only three times. I've found that working with Sherry Anshara by phone for as little as 10 minutes, at other times for a full hour, has resulted in completely resolving inter-current headaches that previously I would have medicated.

Sherry Anshara's work appears to me to combine elements of "energy work", the part that is least understood by our current sciences, somato-emotional release, guided visualization, physical manipulation, which appears to be entirely intuitive on her part since she has had no formal training in this, and affirmations. One could certainly say that it is a form of psycho-neuro-immunology (PNI).

PNI is a major subject of scientific research, which studies the connections between the psyche (cognitive and emotional function) with the brain and the immune system, such as how stress triggers neurons in the hypothalamus (a part of the brain), which affects the pituitary gland (the master gland of the endocrine system which regulates the thyroid and adrenal glands), and how the hormones produced by these glands affect the immune system.

I have also been able to discontinue anti-viral medications, which I had used off and on for years for migrating post-herpetic neuralgias to which I had also applied a host of integrative medicine interventions, but still often required medications such as acyclovir.

Sherry Anshara's process helped me to get to the root of the initial cause of headaches that started forty years ago and release what she terms "destructive cellular memorization patterns", replacing them with healthy "cellular memory".

What I learned about the headaches is that they were triggered by an accident at age 19 when I was doing a back flip off a diving board and hit the board on the bridge of my nose on my way to the water. The headaches started about a year later, triggered both by environmental chemical exposure and by psychological stress. As the headaches became more frequent, my body "memorized" these patterns, which became progressively re-enforced in a negative feedback loop.

The way out of them has been to learn to expand my body's energy field and to replace cellular memorization with the cellular memory that existed prior to the accident at age 19 when I didn't experience headaches. I've learned that when I am under stress, my body's energy field constricts and the dysfunctional cellular memorization kicks in. As I've learned to consciously maintain an expanded energy field, which I do via a process of visualization and breathing that I've learned from Sherry Anshara, and invoke my pre-accident cellular memory, the same stress doesn't precipitate headaches.

Headaches and other health problems such as allergies, asthma, chronic skin fungal infections (athlete's foot), and fatigue all led me into integrative medicine. I learned that improved nutrition and therapies, such as cranial-sacral osteopathy which I first received and then studied in 1979, dramatically improved how I felt. Sherry Anshara's work has been a major piece on this journey of study and learning.

I have also asked Sherry Anshara to work with cancer patients of mine, knowing that she has previously had success in this arena, sometimes with dramatic tumor reduction over periods as short as a week, and have found her work to be extremely useful in this arena as well.

I believe that Sherry Anshara's body of work, called the QuantumPathic® Energy Method, can greatly assist individuals with deep-rooted emotional and/or physical issues. From what I have experienced and seen, it repeatedly works when other methods have resulted in little or no long-term resolution.

I am grateful that others are studying with Sherry Anshara. A good deal of what she has intuitively learned appears to be teachable and transferable to others. It is quite unique in my experience. Probably no one will ever be quite as good at it as Sherry Anshara herself, but 80% of what she is able to do can provide many people with great benefits.

I think that both medical and non-medical practitioners could learn to implement Sherry Anshara's work. The problem with medical practitioners is that they have busy practices, and it takes time and practice to become proficient with the QuantumPathic® Energy Method.

I believe my friends Sharon and Keith (both cranial osteopaths), who recently took Sherry Anshara's first level workshop, may be able to implement some of the QuantumPathic® Energy Method techniques in their own practices, as it is simply an extension of what they already do. Chiropractors, massage therapists, physical therapists, and psychotherapists are all professional groups which could easily learn and incorporate the QuantumPathic® Energy Method into their practices.

I hope to see further teaching and development of Sherry Anshara's work in the world. It is truly wonderful work and badly needed by many who suffer from a wide range of human maladies.

Body Mind Geometry

by Al Swimmer, Ph.D.

One fine day, Sherry Anshara received a call from a close friend, Roxanne, who told her that she was calling from a local hospital where she was waiting to be operated on, as soon as proper preparations could be made, to remove a serious-looking tumor that had just been discovered during a routine examination. Sherry Anshara immediately canceled her pending commitments and went to the hospital. She facilitated for her friend with a QuantumPathic® Energy Method (QPEM) session, "just to make the operation easier".

The surgeon who was to operate, accompanied by a technician, came in and said to Roxanne, they were going to take a final set of X-rays to determine "exactly where the tumor was located". After completing this task, the surgeon and technician left to process the X-ray films. The surgeon returned in a little while, obviously upset and frustrated. He said, "From the first set of X-rays, I know there was a tumor there, but now the tumor has disappeared!!"

Several years ago, Barbara was one of the people attending Sherry Anshara's course, Intuitive Powers/Practical Applications 1, which then met on Monday evenings. Barbara was an attractive, personable woman. Her left leg and left withered foot were inches shorter than her normal right leg and foot. It was not completely developed. She wore a specially made shoe to keep her leg and foot in balance with her normal leg when she walked.

During the class, the students paired off and alternately acted as client and facilitator. One Monday evening during class, Barbara was my partner. We both had our shoes off sitting in adjoining chairs listening to Sherry Anshara teaching the tools of the QuantumPathic® Energy Method (QPEM). Now it was time to assist each other. During the session between me and Barbara, something extraordinary happened.

All of a sudden, her shorter leg lengthened. She stood up, and both legs and feet were in alignment. Everyone in the room, including me, watched as Barbara's left leg and withered foot metamorphosed into almost a normal leg and foot! All of us witnessed this "miracle". We gathered around Barbara to see that indeed her left leg and foot were now in alignment with her right leg and foot. Barbara was, of course, amazed at what had just happened and didn't quite know what to do.

Barbara said she had to put her shoes on. Remember, one of her shoes was specially made so she could stand straight as though both of her legs and feet were even. As she picked up her specially made shoe, everyone watched as her leg and foot shrunk back into a shorter leg and a withered shape. What happened? Everyone witnessed Barbara's innate natural ability to heal herself; however, her irrational Duality Belief Systems (B.S.) that she would always be crippled took over. Her leg shrunk and her foot withered. This is what happens when your limited Belief Systems overcome believing in yourself. You are programmed to Belief System that you cannot heal yourself. Barbara's Belief Systems were that she could not heal her imperfection. The funny thing that happened after her experience in the class is that her leg and foot changed. In fact, she had to have a new shoe made because her leg and foot had actually extended. Her old shoe was too high.

Her leg and foot were not completely "normal", but the "difference" was not as pronounced. The physical and emotional issues of her calf were that she could not stand for her Truth and had to accept that she would always be a "cripple". This was a significant change for her at the cellular level. Barbara was not only healing the structure of her leg and foot, but she was healing the emotional issues of being a cripple.

I assisted Sherry Anshara for several years in the Intuitive Powers/Practical Applications 1 classes. I became accustomed to observing incredible practical miracles happen. Sherry Anshara's QuantumPathic® Energy Method (QPEM) tools support people to heal themselves emotionally and physically at their cellular level within their own bodies. They empower themselves to make the required productive changes that support them to live healthier lives.

I personally benefited from Sherry Anshara's practical magic after I had a heart attack on August 15, 2012. I was taken by ambulance to Banner Desert Hospital that Wednesday morning where a stent was inserted in my leg as an emergency measure. I was scheduled to have a bypass operation on Saturday as soon as my serious condition stabilized. The next day my wife informed Sherry Anshara about my situation, and she came to see me on both Thursday and Friday evenings.

Even after her first visit, my condition improved so much that on Friday the surgeon decided that he could postpone the bypass operation until I had recovered completely, rather than after I was just stabilized from the effects of the heart attack. After Sherry Anshara's visit on Friday evening, there was another major improvement in my condition. I was taken out of the intensive care unit much sooner than usual.

After I was discharged from the hospital, Sherry Anshara came to my house and gave me a third session. My quick recovery and improvement in my health were due to Sherry Anshara's simple but subtle QuantumPathic® Energy Method (QPEM).

My recovery had progressed to such an extent that just a few weeks later, I was able to travel to Portland, Oregon to attend and give two talks at the annual MATHFEST meeting. There were over 1600 mathematicians gathered for 4 days to discuss various mathematical topics.

Sherry Anshara's QuantumPathic® Energy Method (QPEM) teaches people, not only how to heal themselves of physical problems, but more importantly, to heal their emotional and mental issues which had prevented them from becoming the person they were meant to be.

In my observation, the QuantumPathic® Energy Method (QPEM) consists of four major steps: Discovery, Assessment, Connection, and Observation. Each of which, in sequential order, guides one to become the Golden Example that was their potential at birth. Through the QuantumPathic® Energy Method (QPEM), Sherry Anshara has crystallized a universal method that will guide the entire world to external and internal peace and transcendent Beingness.

There is a wonderful book by Deepak Chopra called *Quantum Healing*, (1989). There is a wonderful book by Richard Gordon called *Quantum Touch*, (1999). Besides these, there are no doubt many others over the centuries who have discovered that the internal Quantum Energy possessed by everyone can be harnessed into assisting ourselves and others to a better life.

One might ask the question: Why were Deepak, Richard, Sherry Anshara, and several others all inspired to use the word "Quantum" to describe the mystical experiences that are involved in the healing miracles provided through the tools they teach?

In Deepak Chopra's book, he describes in a fascinating explanation that in physics there is a mysterious realm in which a remarkable transition takes place of a non-material wave of light which somehow can make manifest a material particle, a photon. The word "Quantum" derives from "quanta" which the physicists use to describe the smallest unit which can be called particle-like. There is this mystical process where the vibratory non-material wave becomes a teeny, tiny particle.

In the self-healing process, just as in all thought, a similar process takes place. The non-material thought process of an individual, when guided and supported by someone like Sherry Anshara, creates a physical change. The physical changes begin to occur in both the computer/brain and the body.

The intelligence and intellect is in the body. The limited Duality programs are imprinted in the computer/brain. When the computer/brain is running the emotional issues, sickness is manifested in the body. The computer/brain and the body are disconnected.

During the healing process, a transitional phase occurs from the non-material Quantum world to the material world. As the body consciously awakens through self-healing, the non-material becomes material.

I am not here to give technical explanations or provide beautiful contemplations of the gift of GOD. Yet, everyone has their own innate healing abilities within themselves when they are ready to connect to the Quantum Field within themselves.

Sherry Anshara's QuantumPathic® Energy Method (QPEM) tools support you to connect with the innate and natural God consciousness within you. Then healing at the cellular level within you takes place.

TRANSITIONS

"Involve, revolve, evolve,
or do the involve, revolve again
and don't evolve!

Or Evolve!"

-Sherryism

Quantum Transitions

by Wind Ohmoto

When you become conscious,
you become the space in between which is vastness.

Endurance, Perseverance, Tolerance. This is what it says *Shinobu* means in the Japanese baby name book under boys' names. What?! *Shinobu* was the stage name offered to me decades ago when I performed traditional Japanese dance. Turns out it is an androgynous name. Not pretty sounding, which is what I desired, but I thought it would serve as a good focus for me at the time. Of course I did.

I did not realize I had been setting my Self up to sacrifice and sabotage my life by *enduring, persevering* and *tolerating* life's whatevers. I did not know that I have the Power and the freedom to enjoy the richness and vastness of whatever my Heart desires.

So *unconsciously*, I withdrew my Presence from the Moment, shut down my real intelligence—my body's intuitive feelings—and stayed hidden inside my head. I analyzed and judged my countless short-comings and set out to 'fix' what was never broken. I did not realize that the real issue was the *disconnection* from my Self. And that it was my misguided *thinking* which was making things complicated and confusing.

As a young child, I believed that by having less I would learn to appreciate what little I had all the more. I was valuing the *lack* outside of me. With this non-deserving belief, of course I experienced loss!

After one of my first grade friends stole my Easter gift from my bedroom, she lied to my Mom about it, saying that I had given it to her. In shock, I said nothing. As a result of this incident, I couldn't trust that any of my personal treasures would be safe. Better to value things which cannot be taken away from me, such as knowledge, experiences, and thoughts. These intangibles relied upon my memory.

I had a good memory. It was so good in my idea that I thought I could even bet my life on it. Then one day I discovered my infallible memory was very fallible. Oh no! Now what can I trust?

I clutched onto spirituality…once again giving away my Power.

My Self-analyzing and Self-criticizing further fragmented and alienated me from my Truth. I was not aware that I did not have to prove my worth to anyone…not even to my Self. I was so unaware that *my* value is priceless, and that the Allness of Me is pure magnificence! Who would imagine that my authentic Self is LIFE itself?!! I certainly had no clue!

I did not believe that I could trust my body's intuitive feelings and my Heart, without any doubt. Trusting my Self would have made LIFE crystal clear and easy.

BUT the 'easy' way was just not acceptable to me. I believed 'easy' would be a 'cop-out'. I believed in *enduring* the 'hard' lessons. I believed that if the pain of the lesson was deeply ingrained in me, I would never have to repeat it again, because I'd definitely remember it.

What Belief System (B.S.) was I selling my Self?!! 'No pain no gain'?!! Did I enroll in the 'school of hard knocks'?!! Wow. I set my Self up for pain and struggle!! I did not see that the word 'lived' spelled backwards is 'devil'. Indeed, I was suffering because I was my own 'devil'!

What is the point of *settling for less* and *suffering* all the more, time and time again? I shouldered responsibilities which weren't mine to take on, even financial obligations, *unconsciously* believing this would somehow prove I'm a 'good' person?!! Who was I trying to convince? And WHY?!!!

I created quite the drama! Casting all the actors in the roles of parents, friends, boyfriends, ex-husband, doctors, co-workers, bosses, and even auditors in yet another storyline of financial, emotional, mental, and physical *o-woe-is-me* victimhood. "And the best actor award goes to *all* my Childish Adult Egos who kept the story never-ending AND the Truth ever so elusive."

To decipher my life, I read self-help books, psychic phenomena books, spirituality books, quantum physics books, and more. I took psychology classes. I tried religions. I even became an ordained minister. I tried and studied all sorts of healing modalities. I became a Reiki master and taught Reiki; I learned and taught EFT (Emotional Freedom Technique). You get the idea. I began to wonder if it was possible to get completely free and clear in this lifetime.

My circuitous search ended when I met Sherry Anshara in November 2009. The sheer brilliance of her QuantumPathic® Energy Method (QPEM) was powerful beyond anything I had ever experienced. Through QPEM, I discovered that I am far more powerful than I ever imagined.

The QuantumPathic® Energy Method (QPEM) is direct, to the point, and it makes *real* practical sense. No one does anything *to* me or *for* me. It's *with* my participation. The QPEM supports me to connect *with* my Self and to be in charge of my own healing.

I am so grateful that I created the opportunity to become free and clear by writing Sherry Anshara into my script. I did not know that she would be my ticket out of the Fear Programs of Duality! I didn't even know what that meant.

I LOVE LIFE and I LOVE ME!! I am *complete* with all the no-senseness. I now consciously choose expansiveness every day and being connected with *Heartness*, the pure essence of my Heart, enjoying the Newness I'm creating in my miraculous life!

So what exactly happened? Let's visit my time continuum.

As a young child I was resentful that I had been born. I didn't see any point. Being a child was hard enough and I believed life only got more complicated the older you got. Too much responsibility!

Dad, a.k.a. Henry, was enduring life in misery, according to my perception. Most of his adult life he worked as a gardener, just like his brother and his father. He worked long hours six days a week in his responsible role as our breadwinner. And on Sunday, his only 'day off', he worked on our yard.

One Sunday, as Dad was working in our backyard, I cheerfully asked if I could help him. He laughed and said it would make him happier if I did the dishes for Mom instead. Dad didn't see that all I wanted was to spend some one-on-one time with him. How could he know? I never spoke the words to tell him. I just went inside quietly and washed the dishes like a 'good girl'...totally rejected in my idea. My unexpressed disappointment stayed stuck in my throat, manifesting later as chronic pains in my neck and jaw. The k**nots** of ***not*** being able to speak my Truth continued to grow in number year after year.

Dad worked *hard* for decades as a gardener and understandably got burned out. He was stuck without any viable options, so he *endured, persevered,* and *tolerated* gardening. I told my Self that I was NOT going to be stuck like him in a job. No way!

On television, I watched an interview which showed me it was possible to *LOVE* working. The famous actress being interviewed disclosed that she so enjoyed discovering the depths of her Self through her characters that she would even act without getting paid for it.

Wow! A fulfilling life with no money worries! What a lovely dream. It did *not* match my reality. It did *not* match my *unconscious* investment in *lack*. My *lack* of comprehension regarding my own *value* and *worth* and *deservingness*. And in *lack* there is no fulfillment.

My 'normal' was to *enryo*. '*Enryo*', in the Japanese language, means to refrain from one's desires and defer to others out of politeness. I would always say and do what I thought I was supposed to.

Here is an early example of this. While on a play date with my first grade classmate, we walked by a vacant lot which surprisingly had a rocket ship. I could see how much he wanted to explore it. I had no interest. I told him to go and play with the other kids because I was really 'okay' standing where I was. I told him I would wait. However, I desperately wished he would *enryo* and pick me instead. He never did hear my inner pleading thoughts of "please, PLEASE…don't go, don't go, DON'T GO!!!" So he went.

He bought my *enryo* lie. I could not speak my Truth. I stood there for what seemed an eternity, watching him have fun on the rocket ship with the other kids. The wind kicked up and blew dust across the vacant lot. Abandoned in my idea, I started crying. A couple of older girls walking by saw me crying and became concerned. Embarrassed and ashamed that I was caught being a 'crybaby', I tried to speak, but all I could do was cry even more. The girls walked me home. And I abandoned my classmate.

I kept repeating this scenario of not speaking my Truth without ever learning to honor my own Heart's desires first and foremost. Why? I was running a 'good girl' program, which puts others first. This Belief System really wasn't 'good' for me…or 'okay'. Yet I continued to *enryo.* And I continued to give away my Power. I became a master at re-creating the victim-victimizer role.

Remember the television interview with the actress? I kept telling my Self that I would someday find something I absolutely loved to do, just like her. Yet I ended up getting a job as a clerk typist.

I came home with a horrible headache after the first day of work. My body was saying, "No, this isn't working for me." But I told my Self, "I would look like a flake on my resume if I quit too soon." I also recalled that Dad said I was a 'quitter' a while back when I announced I was going to start running every day. In my idea, he didn't believe I could persevere. I'd prove him wrong. So I decided to endure the job for just one year, and then I would find something I truly enjoyed. This is the promise I made to my Self.

For over 35 years, I forced my Self to *endure*, *persevere*, and *tolerate* jobs at that company, never quitting. I tried to suppress my underlying discontent. It was exhausting.

The lovely promise I made to my Self to do something I truly loved kept getting postponed to the next year until I ended up just like Dad. How did I let this happen?!!

Tolerate the intolerable and survive until death. Oh such fun. I had no clue that I was afraid I was not acceptable to me. And this is what I kept enduring…my fear of not being good enough. What is 'enough'?

I desperately wanted my Dad's verbal approval. I wanted him to say: "I am proud of you." So I gave away my Power *unconsciously* as I hooked my Self into the Self-sabotage invalidation cycle to validate him.

According to Sherry Anshara, this 'affliction' is not unique in the least. Seeking validation is at the very core of addiction. We are so afraid of being abandoned and rejected…again…that we will invalidate our Selves to validate the invalidation that the 'authority figure' is doing to get his or her approval! Of course, this doesn't resolve anything. Hence the cycle continues regardless of whether that 'authority figure' is still in your life or not!

In other words, I was the one who made me as miserable and as stuck as I perceived Dad to be, just to get his approval. I was seeking validation from a person who probably was not feeling validated him Self!

Would anything have changed if Dad had said those 'magic' words, "I'm proud of you"? No!! I was running a deeply embedded fear program which had nothing to do with him. It was all about me. The one who was afraid of *not being good enough* or *worthy* was me! Through the QuantumPathic® Energy Method (QPEM), I would discover the *unconscious* belief that **I do not deserve to live**. It was imprinted in my cellular memory. Where did this Self-punishment program come from?

The Shift Begins

The Non-Emotional Observer (NEO) is the beginning of *natural* behavior. It is the opportunity to be your *natural*

> Real Self. You are not hooked into the un*natural*ness of emotions. Emotions are "normal" in Duality. They are NOT *natural* to your Soul.
>
> *-Wind*

In November 2009, I participated in my first QuantumPathic® course on my actual birthday. It was the BEST birthday gift I had ever given to my Self! Once I got out of my head, I was able to connect to my cellular memories as a Non-Emotional Observer (NEO) to get information to facilitate my healing without re-traumatizing my Self.

With my inner sight, I saw scenes from my lifetimes after lifetimes of war, war, and more war, and being a warrior/soldier time and time again, through the facilitation of fellow students. It was my body's intelligence revealing to me an imprinted pattern of war and conflict and giving away my Power. I could finally comprehend the senselessness of it all.

In one of the imprinted warrior memories, I saw clearly the image of a very young, terrified Viking boy. He was me. We had been ordered to kill everybody in the village, including women and children. It was horrific. The Viking boy had to survive it so he dared not to feel. He killed helpless people…for his own survival…and he sacrificed his own humanity.

I do not deserve to live is a belief I had been unconsciously running ever since that lifetime. The puzzling pieces of my life were beginning to make sense. No wonder I created a Self-punishment program! I was still the victimizer victimizing my own Self for something I had done…how many lifetimes ago?! How relevant is it to me here in this Moment now?

I was eager to release this non-supportive belief and I did so by taking back my Power and taking charge of my life! I do deserve to live! I do deserve to feel! I do deserve to be alive! In that Moment, I could *feel* the aliveness of my body for the very first time in my life! This day became the ***real*** birth day of **me**.

I learned that getting to the origination points of my issues gives me the opportunity to clear them. This is where the real healing takes place, at the core where it began. In 10 minutes or less I can connect to my body's cellular intelligence to get the *relevant* information. When the imprinted experience supports me, I make a conscious choice to keep the *resonance* and expand upon it. When it does not support me, I let it go. This frees me to fully engage in the experiences which are happening in this Moment, without re-triggering emotionality and limiting belief patterns from the past.

Thanks to the QuantumPathic® Energy Method (QPEM), I released lifetimes of B.S. (Belief Systems) from my cellular memory. My value and worth to me grew. I no longer was willing to put my body through any more suffering.

Now that I cared about me and loved me, I chose to give my new best friend—ME!—a fabulous birthday gift. Retirement from the company!! YAY!! It wasn't doable the year before. But my savings/retirement fund had been steadily increasing to double the amount in just one year! My own personal value had been appreciating as well. Fascinating how our creativity works, isn't it?

I orchestrated an *easy* work transition right after my department was reorganized. In my first meeting with my new manager, which was two days before my 60th birthday, I officially announced my retirement plans and recommended my replacement. Her response was humorous: "Wow!! I don't know you or I'd say I'll miss you!"

It's interesting to observe that my work responsibilities had always been about following and enforcing policies and regulations. My only expression of creativity in work was within those parameters, and it was only to make the processes more efficient and automated. My own personal objective was to eliminate my job tasks. And ultimately I succeeded. BUT…what did it cost me? A LOT!! I suppressed my own voice…my own Heart…my creative Power. I sacrificed my life.

All that limitedness was now over, and it was my time to fully embrace life and to enjoy my own creative expressions. However, along with all the freedom, laughter, fun, and pure joy I was newly experiencing, my body was still in a lot of pain.

For years, my body had been breaking down from repeatedly forcing my Self to re-create and re-create the same non-supportive behavior day after day. I found out I even had a torn rotator cuff. Now what do I do? Clear out all the Duality imprinting from my body is what!!! Then my body has the opportunity to heal itself.

During a private QuantumPathic® Energy Method (QPEM) session with Sherry Anshara, she intuited information from my body about a lifetime I had in Japan. And I saw a photographic-like image of a military officer, but he was not Japanese. He looked European. Through the assistance of the internet, I discovered that the man I saw was Lieutenant Colonel Charles Antoine Marquerie, original chief of the second French military mission to Japan in 1872.

Japan was engaged in an internal power struggle as they transitioned away from the Samurai culture. The new Japanese Emperor brought in the French military to assist in reorganizing and training the Imperial Japanese army and establishing the first military service draft law. Marquerie. He is who I was. And who was the Japanese Emperor? Sherry Anshara.

It's interesting to me that I chose to be Japanese in my next lifetime…and that I chose French as my college major in my current lifetime. That next lifetime surfaced in another session with Sherry Anshara.

'Japan 1290' is what Sherry Anshara got from my body; while I saw an image of a highly decorated short man in a military uniform superimposed over an old map of Nagasaki, the name *Yamamoto,* and then the name *Musashi.*

At first we assumed 1290 was a year. Checking the internet revealed that 1290 was the number of days between the bombing of Pearl Harbor and the atomic bombing of Nagasaki. It was the number of days that the Japanese-Americans were in internment camps in the United States. And my parents in my current lifetime were interned in the camps during World War II.

The man I had seen was Admiral Isoroku Yamamoto, commander and chief responsible for Pearl Harbor and the Battle of Midway. The super-battleship *Musashi* was the name of his flagship, which he was against constructing. It was commissioned into service at *Nagasaki.* Yamamoto's cremated remains were transported back to Tokyo on the *Musashi.*

Through the internet I learned that Yamamoto had studied at Harvard and was fluent in English and was strongly opposed to the war with the U.S. But he did his duty for the Emperor and his nation. He was a target of death threats by both Japanese nationalists and Americans. He died when his plane was shot down over the South Pacific after his itinerary was intercepted and *decrypted* by American Naval Intelligence.

Interestingly, in my current lifetime I worked in *Information Security* at a major aerospace defense contractor for many years. And Yamamoto was particularly interested in naval aviation. I see how the career I ended up creating was not so random after all.

A recent program I saw on television stated that Yamamoto died before the end of World War II, but I know his internal war continued on inside of me. I entered my current lifetime resisting life, resisting my Self. War is hell.

"You pick up where you left off." I've heard Sherry Anshara say this countless times. But I finally got the **Inner Truth** of 'it' as the timelines in my body began to merge. Nothing had significantly changed no matter how many lifetimes of opportunities I have had to create real Newness. The infinity symbol ∞ is the symbol of the same old same old continuous loop of Duality's ups and downs. Being 'creative' within Duality is just changing places, faces, genders, and races, but the stories, the experiences, are just a continuation.

By utilizing my cellular memory from relevant lifetimes as a valuable tool, I comprehend without a doubt that one lifetime continues on into the next. ***"You pick up where you left off."*** Yamamoto was very vocal about his thoughts and highly visible. All it got him were death threats from Japanese nationalists and shot and killed by Americans. So in my current lifetime, I tried to be quiet and invisible, which did not work out well either.

We were both running sacrifice programs. We sacrificed our Selves each time we gave away our Power to whomever or whatever was "above" us in our idea. We betrayed and abandoned our Selves. And the *projection* of betrayal and abandonment naturally attracts to us betrayers as a perfect *match* in the dysfunctional *resonance* of non-support. Our internal war gets projected outward into these relationships. This is how we create and support Duality lifetime after lifetime.

Imprinted and programmed by parents, teachers, clergy, doctors, and the media, it may seem that the only way out of the Duality boxes of limitation is death. Some people may think, "I'll just die and everything will be okay again." BUT, death is the punch-line of the Belief System joke that we keep falling for lifetime after lifetime. When we use death as an escape from Duality, we have just bought a round-trip ticket back to Trauma-Drama-World. **Until we get conscious, nothing changes.** The joke is on us!

And if you are ready for this, I'll share with you that lifetimes are not linear. We are multi-dimensional Beings, which allows us to have multiple experiences and lifetimes simultaneously. With this comprehension, additional puzzling pieces dissipated for me.

My body has been assisting me to transition out of Duality while still in this human form in this lifetime. I released Yamamoto's grief, sadness, and regret, which were still stored in my cellular memory. I released the resonance of *pathetic.* This is not a judgment. It's a frequency and vibration of Duality. Sherry Anshara personally witnessed the word *pathetic* release out of my body along with that frequency and vibration.

My unconscious lifetimes became my own Groundhog Day movie. I became a master of Duality do-overs and do-it-agains. I am gratefully *complete* with all that now. No more roles for me!

How exhausting and boring and pathetic!!! No more shutting my Self down or up.

How do I spell relief? G-e-t-t-i-n-g C-o-n-s-c-i-o-u-s

With gratitude to my Self, I continue to create the opportunities to dissolve all of Duality from the inside out!

Creating Newness

After I cleared the need for validation, I was able to experience an entirely new relationship with Dad. He made it a point to visit me in Arizona regularly. He gave me one-on-one times with him!! I realize it now. What a beautiful gift of connection and completion.

Once I stopped projecting the daughter role, I was able to connect *with* him, not as a daughter to a father or as one role to another role, but as one magnificent, unique Human Being *with* another magnificent, unique Human Being. And we were able to connect in new, wondrous ways.

It is so amazing to me that Dad actually said the 'magic' words to me, "I am proud of you", last year and it didn't matter at all. I truly do not require external validation anymore. YAY!

Last year, as I drove Dad to the airport at the end his visit, he announced: "I'm going to sing you a song." What Newness! He sang 'Oh What a Beautiful Morning' from the musical *Oklahoma.* All the verses!

Dad then surprised me again by revealing, "I'm going to sing another song." It was 'It Might as Well Be Spring' from the musical *State Fair.* My eyes became teary. I felt so deeply moved. With the pure sincerity of my Heart, I said to him, "You sang better than Frank Sinatra."

I was not aware Dad could sing so well. He said he used to sing with his friends when he was young, but I never heard him sing while I was growing up, not even once. He said he only sang to Mom one time. It was in the car as he was driving her home from the hospital for the last time after her terminal diagnosis, and she cried while he sang.

My Dad, this 90-year-old man, remembered all the lyrics, and he sang with such confidence and ease. Those two songs from his Heart were the greatest gifts he could have given to me. **Pure Heartness.** He performed an encore for me the last time he visited. **Pure Joy.**

I was on the phone with my sister Phyllis when she said goodnight to Dad for the last time. I was on the phone with her the next day when she went to awaken him. He wasn't responding. Phyllis was very calm as she said softly to me, "I think he's gone." He transitioned unexpectedly. He was not ill. I was with Phyllis on the phone while the paramedics were there and she shared with me that she was choosing not to blame her Self at all. So conscious!

With compassion and comprehension, Phyllis realizes that Dad left the way he desired, quickly and cleanly without prolonged illness. His girlfriend had been ill for many years and wasn't even recognizing him. She passed away just 2 months before. Whatever he felt he owed her was now complete. Dad had been very clear he was not going to die that way. And he didn't!

Two days before he left this lifetime, we chatted on the phone. He requested the lyrics to the song 'You'll Never Walk Alone' from the musical *Carousel.* I had given him those lyrics recently, but he asked for them again. What a huge clue and what a message.

In the same phone conversation, I opened the funny musical birthday card Dad had recently given to me. The card said: "You aren't old until the fat lady sings." Inside a hefty Brünnhilde belts out: "AAAAAAAAAAAAAAHHHHHHHHH"!! It was so funny to me and to him. We both laughed with joy. Of course the actual saying is, "It ain't over until the fat lady sings" and we both heard her sing. Dad's role in this 'opera' was just about over.

He was complete with his life. Phyllis and I both comprehend this without a single doubt, that he created his transition without drama, without illness, without a long process of suffering. Bravo, Dad! You did it your way! What a Master you are!

Our responses to Dad's transition have demonstrated to me that we are progressively evolving beyond Duality. Phyllis and I realize that there are many people who may have resisted what happened, stayed in shock, attached to the past, grieving the loss, 'wishing' he was still here. We've learned that 'loss' is no longer in our vocabulary. Henry (Dad) is creating Newness experiences for him Self.

We continue to appreciate him. We continue to radiate our love and support with Heartness, cheering him onward. Every day I connect *with* all the cells, molecules, and particles in my body, where my *real* intelligence resides. And I radiate expansive Heartness to Henry, Phyllis, and to every Being on this planet.

Phyllis and I are not choosing to 'miss' Dad. He is not missing. He moved on to his Newness and that assists us to create our own Newness. We connect *with* each other…Heartness to Heartness. We *honor* Life and Realness. We are actualizing our Transition out of Duality with gratitude and appreciation.

Ohmoto is my Dad's last name and mine. It means 'Great Source'. What a clear clue that the real Power Source of my Life is *me.* Multi-dimensional ME! I get it now! By grounding my Presence in this human body in this Moment, I *feel* alive. I am experiencing what is actually happening right now…without any references to the past or the future. By connecting and listening *with* my multi-dimensional Beingness, my experiences are exciting, powerful, and efficient. Moments flow with ease and joy because I'm not stopping the flow by thinking. The Real Transition for me is Being LIFE in this expansive, continuous, continuing Moment. My Ho**ME** is in this Moment.

In the midst of making preparations for the service to celebrate Dad's life, I assisted participants in the QuantumPathic® Healing Your Core intensive workshop. Supporting individuals on this planet to get conscious and free of fear—which is simply a lack of information—is of the utmost importance to me.

This past weekend I assisted in another QuantumPathic® Healing Your Core workshop. I am amazed at how the comprehension of participants in these workshops have accelerated and deepened over the years. Without resisting their Selves, they easily access clear information from the cellular memories in their bodies pertaining to their issues. And just as easily, they free their Selves of the embedded traumas and non-supportive Belief Systems. In this workshop, I observed one participant's joy burst into laughter and the BEST happy dancing I've ever seen! She was *feeling* fully alive!

I comprehend now that **Life is easy**. Duality is hard. Life is the opportunity to experience the unlimited fullness of our Selves. And to enjoy each other…resonating, connecting, sharing, and creating Newness experiences with ease and joy! How FUNtastic is this?!

In connecting *with* my body's intelligence, my experiences are multi-dimensional, fun, and miraculous. Feeling and trusting my Heart, my inner dimensions are merging and the voice of my Soul is emerging.

As I continue to learn and expand in my progressive process, I feel even more free and sovereign. More and more individuals are connecting *with* me in the Moment, and we communicate in *real* conversations without scripted words being spoken. *Real*ationships. Allness is a**WE**so**ME**!

Every single person involved in their own conscious evolution makes a profound difference to so many others as they interact and connect with people every Moment. As parents become conscious and in charge of their lives, they are able to support their children to believe in their Selves without the imprinting of limited beliefs.

Can you imagine parents having Heartness-to-Heartness conversations with their child? Actively listening *with* their Hearts to their child without projecting their own fears, expectations, and dreams? Wow! Being able to speak your Truth as a child and being acknowledged! What a difference this could make in the entire family dynamics and in relationships. What a difference this could make in the global dynamics of humanity.

Instead of imagining all this, let's take action…NOW! By making Heartness-to-Heartness connections, we experience Realness! By completing our own internal war, we stop projecting conflict and opposition into our outer experiences. And as we radiate peacefulness from all the cells of our body, we contribute to the global Shift out of Duality! And this is just the beginning of our Quantum Transitions to our own Vastness!!

I am the deepening Presence of my Soul in this human body experiencing this Moment with the pure essence of my Heart… *Heartness!* I choose to expand my resonance consciously and intentionally. I activate the Akyra Zynanda god particle of pure creation and love in the heart of every cell of my body and resonate with the Fenon Field of Non-Duality. And I create each of my experiences in the Moment…trusting my feelings and my intuition and my Power! I create ease and flow and new words to express it such as *flowductive* (flow + productive) and *flowtivity* (flow + creativity).

I am Expansiveness.

I am Joy.

I am the Multi-verse.

I am Life itself!

I am Me.

Currently, Wind is a joyful expression of her creativity, and she is collaborating with a team of conscious individuals to deliver Sherry Anshara's information globally.

A Moment in Time

by Donna Sparaco

I was a middle child. I'm not sure if that had anything to do with my "average" mentality. I was also tall so I always sat or stood in the back. As a "C" student, it seemed only right to take my place in society's lineup.

I had tenacity, though. That's immeasurable. Why then, was it that I never thought I could reach the heights I was looking for? What was holding me back?

I remember it like it was yesterday. I was wearing a dress. It was 1st grade and I liked school. Well, mostly. At this moment, my stomach was in knots and I was trying to hold back tears that were gliding down my cheeks.

To say I was mortified is an understatement. I wanted to shrink into oblivion as I watched this short, stocky, grey-haired lady grab the chalk and waddle up to the blackboard. In an effort to create a visual for me, she proceeded to draw an apple as big as she could to demonstrate what happens when half of it is eaten.

If I couldn't grasp the concept of fractions, how was I going find out how fractions worked now? I lost hope and desire to learn, as I sat there feeling like an idiot. My brain froze and I didn't dare ask her about it ever again. They say it doesn't hurt to ask, but that day it hurt.

It became a moment frozen in time of shame and angst. This moment I would carry with me until I met Sherry Anshara some 50 odd years later.

Growing up, I consciously worked hard to improve myself. I always felt like the "Little Engine that Could". Down deep I knew I could achieve success, but always seemed to stop short when it came to my financial achievements. The glass lid that everyone talks about was definitely hovering above my head.

When I was in my 20's, I actually remember saying I didn't want to make good money because I wasn't interested in working long hours and didn't want to be responsible. WHAT? I now know that I was afraid to find out if I truly was stupid. In reality I was always responsible.

Even as a young boy, my brother was always comfortable with money. I was afraid of it. He understood what seemed like a complicated secret to me, and I was in awe of his relationship with it.

As I got older, I wondered why it seemed so easy for some to achieve financial success and impossible for others. I knew I could do anything I put my mind to, so what was the problem? Something as simple as generating six figures was out of my reach.

In an effort to improve my potential, I took courses, went to psychics, healers, palm readers, life coaches and counselors. I always read personal development books and listened to CDs of the same.

I spent the best part of 30 years working on "peeling the layers of the onion" to make room for all possibilities of growth, understanding, awareness and knowledge. Truth be told, I didn't focus on financial gain until I was in my late 40's. By that time, a lot of great groundwork had been laid, but the lifestyle I was after continued to elude me.

I'd been a Girl Scout until I was a senior in high school and always loved helping people. It made sense then that I always looked for customer service jobs, which would have nothing to do with numbers.

That was great but I started to look for something that would feed my soul as well as generate the income I desired. I wanted to do good while doing well. I had no idea what I was looking for until I discovered LegalShield.

This ridiculously low cost legal plan offers everyone across the nation the chance to speak to an attorney about his or her problems, big or small! This was a dream come true! I found a way to help the masses! It was magical. Why then, was I still stuck?

As I look back, I realize all the decisions in my life consisted of strategic activity that didn't require math. When my husband wanted to know what kind of money we would make with this company, I told him I had no idea.

There were so many layers to building an organization similar to that of a real estate or insurance brokerage, that I found it difficult to explain it. I reminded him I wasn't a numbers person. I told him he could call our sponsor to see how the commission and residual income worked. This frustrated him to no end and although I could totally see why, I was unable to answer his question.

You might even say the success of my failure was simply because I could not see the target.

One day, feeling completely vulnerable, I confessed my inadequacies to my brother. His response blew me away. "Of course we're 'C' students, Donna. We're entrepreneurs." Incredible! He was so nonchalant and matter-of-fact; I just had to believe him. Right then, ever so slightly, I started to view myself differently. I am so grateful for that powerful, albeit short conversation.

Fast forward a few years to when my accountability coach, Traci Bogan, called and said, "I know what's holding you back! I met this woman because I stumbled into her workshop. She spoke to me like she was expecting me. Right now, call Sherry Anshara and tell her you need to change your money belief!"

WOW. I wasted no time! My desire to achieve more would only manifest if I was willing to take action.

That first session with Sherry Anshara was life changing! Releasing. Hopeful. As instructed, I told her why I was there. She assisted me in seeing a repeated pattern that could not be denied. The problem? I had no idea how to stop the cycle.

This session was like a massage, but instead of silence there was conversation. I was caught in a web of repeating what I perceived to be my parents' story. In that first hour, I learned to release their story and their Belief Systems around money. I can't say I completely understood what it meant to release something on a "cellular level", but something changed because my business started to grow within weeks. I was on my way.

A few weeks after that session, I had the opportunity to enroll in the QuantumPathic® Healing Your Core workshop. This 20-hour workshop opened my eyes and my heart, as well as my mind. Even if I didn't feel a change right away, those around me did. My actions were deliberate. My attitude was confident. I was focused. How I viewed myself changed.

The proverbial lid was being lifted. In the past, I could only see myself earning $60K a year, but now I could see myself earning $60K a month! Did that change happen with a snap of a finger? Well that depends. It is said it only takes a moment to make a decision, but it can take years to reach that moment. My thought went from "I could never" to "Why not me?" My belief in myself grew exponentially.

During the workshop, Traci and I partnered up for an exercise that required us to face each other and announce our affirmations out loud. I'd done this before. You speak loud and clear, all the ways you envision yourself to be, even if you're not there yet.

I went first. "I AM AN INCREDIBLE MENTOR. I AM A LEADER. I AM AN EXCELLENT MONEY MANAGER. I AM BEAUTIFUL. I AM FUNNY. I AM AN EXECUTIVE DIRECTOR. I AM SUCCESSFUL. I am successful…" It didn't sit too well but I knew one day I would actually believe what I was saying. At that point, I was going through the process. Then it was Traci's turn.

WOW. She was LOUD AND CLEAR AND STRONG! CONFIDENT. This woman believed in herself! As soon as the exercise was over Traci stepped away for a minute, and it hit me like a tidal wave! I let out a baby's cry. I was rebirthing that moment so long ago. I couldn't believe it. I almost doubled over.

"Where is it?" asked Sherry Anshara as she came running over.

"In my gut."

"Who's there?"

"Miss Hogan," I said sobbing as tears were streaming down my face. Dang! That moment in 1st grade was still sitting in my gut so many years later! And so it went with me repeating Sherry Anshara's words, "Knowing at my deepest knowing, I cannot change the past. What I can do is release the past from my cellular memory where it no longer serves me. Miss Hogan had no idea who I was and did the best and the worst with what she knew or didn't know. And in her effort to teach, there was no way that I could know that she was more afraid than me."

This was so simple that it's hard to believe it could actually do anything, let alone increase my business.

I felt better immediately. Calmer. The tug of war inside me stopped.

I cannot pinpoint the precise moment it happened, but I no longer felt stupid. I doubled my income the following month and again the month after that. What changed? My thought? My belief? I was no longer swimming upstream. Don't get me wrong. This isn't magic and it still takes work to achieve goals, but the path was clear.

Unbeknownst to me, the event that took place when I was in 1st grade actually set the course for all decisions I would make moving forward. It's no surprise then that this would include my professional life, as obstacles and insecurities always seemed to circle around money, or lack of.

Sure I was creative, and even witty. Comical and sincere! But I would explain to people that I wasn't smart and it was okay. When I would tell people I wasn't a numbers person, it seemed fine to label myself that way. Truthfully, I never saw the harm in it. I thought I was just being honest. People accepted that definition and so did I.

Not anymore. When I think about how many times I had logically explained what had happened that day in class so long ago, I am amazed to realize that all I really accomplished was to relive and reinforce my inner belief of not being smart enough. Not a numbers person? I knew I wasn't stupid but I certainly didn't think I was smart.

Recently someone emailed me and told me I had an impressive background. I had to sit back and stare at that for a few minutes. No one had ever said that to me. What do you know! I am smart! Not because she told me I was, but because for the first time in my life, I believed it.

I've always loved life, and am once again excited about what the future has in store for my husband and me. Ever since the workshop, I have been able to reach beyond my imaginary average capabilities. I have increased my activity, doing what is required to reach for and achieve my financial goals. Prior to my QuantumPathic® Energy Method (QPEM) experience, I "wished" I was better. Now I am becoming better. My confidence is back. I believe in myself again and most importantly, I no longer make decisions based on that moment when I was a mere child of six.

I now know that I deserve to flourish. What used to be reserved for everyone else is within my reach. I am attracting the people who are as excited and motivated as I am to assist and empower others! I have been officially introduced to the law of attraction.

I can't thank you enough, Sherry Anshara, for what you do.

Today I am free to succeed.

Discovering Your Own Power to Heal

by Marlo Cook

When people ask me about QuantumPathic®, this is what I have to say. The QuantumPathic® Energy Method (QPEM) is the most non-threatening method of getting to the core of emotional and physical issues which I have ever experienced. People ask me, how can that be?

I respond… What made it feel non-threatening to me? It became so evident to me that I did not have to sit in a therapist's office trying and trying to deal with remembering the trauma. When I did this, I sometimes re-lived and re-experienced the traumatic experiences that occurred in my life over and over again. Really? This must be what Post-Traumatic Stress Disorder, PTSD, is…having to re-live the traumas repeatedly in my head. My intention was that I could somehow convey to a particular therapist the Why's and the How's I was experiencing life the way I did. My expectation was that they would provide insight to me by assisting me to get to the bottom of my issues. My goal was they would help me to heal.

After experiencing the QuantumPathic® Energy Method (QPEM), I was astounded. I now had the QPEM tool to discover the Why's and the How's. This is the missing piece of the puzzle to heal myself.

I met Sherry Anshara at a Psychic Fair Expo in my hometown. She was demonstrating the QuantumPathic® Energy Method (QPEM) to the attendees. I figured she was just another psychic...lah dee dah. I was tired and just wanted to go home. I heard her tell her assistant that she was exhausted and please do not to take any more appointments. But she kept taking more people.

The second to last one was my boyfriend. I didn't really think twice about it. This was what he felt he needed. I was hardly paying attention. I was looking around when all of a sudden I heard her tell him he was stuck at age 9. This piqued my interest. She asked him a few more questions and I stepped away to give him some privacy.

While talking with Sherry Anshara's assistant at the booth, I began leafing through her book, *And The Point Is...? Beyond Duality*. I decided to buy it and see what she had to say. I really thought it had a funny name. I figured if she took the time to write and publish something, she must have felt it was worthwhile to get it out to the world.

When I saw she lived in Arizona, I asked myself…"Who and why would anyone come all the way to Ohio to promote whatever this was?" I felt deep inside and said to myself…"there is something going on here."

Sherry Anshara's assistant asked me…"Are you interested in being on our mailing list?" She stated that Sherry Anshara was offering a special promotion. I definitely was interested. So, I signed up.

My boyfriend and I went home. And that was that.

Within the next couple weeks, I picked up Sherry Anshara's book and started to read it. I really liked what I was reading. The issues on Duality, Consciousness, Validation, Belief Systems, Childish Adult Ego, Wanty-needy, etc. made sense to me. The way she put this information together blew me away. Honestly, everything, everything she had to say made sense. I wanted to know more. A couple weeks later I got a call from a woman named Sandy. She asked me if I was interested in attending a workshop Sherry Anshara was having in West Virginia. The timing was right. I was so excited I called to make my payment, forgetting she lived in Arizona. There was a 3-hour time difference between our time zones. Although it was 5 a.m. in Arizona, she was still excited and happy to talk with me. I told Sherry Anshara…"I am looking forward to seeing you in April."

I attended the 4-day QuantumPathic® Energy Method Facilitator Training with about 10 other people. During those 4 days, I witnessed so many breakthroughs for the class participants. Sherry

Anshara shared with us about Third Dimension Duality, our limited Belief Systems, and how our Childish Adult Ego has to participate in our trauma dramas which affect and rule our lives. The key is we must make clear choices to at last grow up into our adult bodies and not stay stuck in the childhood ages of the traumas.

Our Childish Adult Ego, our survivalist, doesn't have to survive the trauma dramas anymore. He or she grows up emotionally, mentally, spiritually, and financially to thrive instead of survive. Our clear adult is in charge of our life.

She continued to explain about the emotional hooks and the bands that we have inside of us stuck at a particular age and stage of our lives. These hooks and bands are the Duality Fear Programs of Judgment, Lack and Take Away.

The interesting thing is that Sherry Anshara teaches us to empower ourselves by letting go of the blame game (b-lame game). Not only stop blaming ourselves, but stop blaming other people for our problems. The tools of the QuantumPathic® Energy Method (QPEM) are not a fix-it solution. You have to do your own work. Your body does the talking and you get to the core of the matter within minutes.

This is what makes it different. The QuantumPathic® Energy Method (QPEM) made all the difference in my life personally and professionally. Yes, people around me noticed the difference. The most important thing is I noticed the difference in how I created my life.

Sherry Anshara's QuantumPathic® Energy Method (QPEM) encourages YOU and teaches YOU how to be the Non-Emotional Observer (NEO). As you implement these tools, you are clearly able to access the information without re-living the pain or trauma, which can be identified as PTSD. The QPEM guides a person to access his or her own cellular memory where he or she is stuck in a traumatic event or situation in his or her past.

With this incredible tool of becoming the Non-Emotional Observer (NEO), which supports you to use your own innate intuition, you can, without judgment, see where the other person or persons are also stuck in the past. In this emotional stuckness of the past, you could say this is the place where your worlds collided in a traumatic event or continuing situations.

One of the most significant tools in the QPEM Facilitator class is learning how to really forgive and even forget. What does this mean? In the old paradigm of forgiveness, there is the caveat that you forgive someone or even yourself, but you still do not forget. When you hold on to the not forgetting, you are not forgiving. You still "hold on" to the past experience. This past experience or experiences are still embedded physically and emotionally in your body at your cellular level. Sherry Anshara teaches that you cannot change the past, but you can release the past emotionally and physically. She says…"The past is one second ago, and the future is one second from now. You can change the future by not dragging the dysfunctional past forward." This is a great place to begin your forgiveness. YOU cannot change the past when you hold on to the dysfunction of the past. It just becomes your future. The date doesn't matter.

Forgiveness for yourself and others frees you to create a healthier future. Remember, the future is only one second from now. It just takes a second. No more guilt or shame or even blame for that matter. As the Non-Emotional Observer (NEO), you give yourself the opportunities to acknowledge the past, to cut the dysfunctional bands physically and emotionally to the past, and free yourself at your cellular level. You release the pain and the discordances in your body.

Before my very eyes I watched several people, including myself, transform their physical bodies with the assistance of Sherry Anshara through the QuantumPathic® Energy Method (QPEM). I witnessed a woman who had a stroke regain movement in her face. Another woman released her back pain which was associated with the sexual abuse that she experienced in her childhood. As a result of her participation in this class, she was able to get off her medication. I also was able to release and heal the terrible back pain that I had experienced for over a year. My pain was from an injury which I was not sure I would ever be able to ever get rid of.

Through my experiences in the class, I also learned that there are no accidents. Believe it or not, I came to understand that we create everything in our lives. The big problem with this concept at first is, how do we do that? How the heck could I have created this accident? Or for that matter, how could anyone create illness, including myself? You can say we do it for the lessons, the karma, or whatever. But the truth is, when we are unconscious, we create these events or situations to wake ourselves up.

As Sherry Anshara states…"Pain in our body is our body's attempt to get our attention. When we suppress the pain with pain pills, medications, or just plain ignore the pain, the body eventually has no choice but to get our attention. This could be through 'illness or an accident'." So you see, we do really create everything in our lives, again without that blame game or self-judgment. We can create the opportunities in our lives to be healthy instead of sick. Becoming conscious is the way.

As I witnessed each person participating in the QuantumPathic® Energy Method (QPEM) process, I realized from the outside we may all look different, but on the inside as human beings we are all having similar experiences. It truly was amazing to see the changes manifesting right before our eyes and how much love and compassion we had for one another.

As each person healed himself or herself on the table, we all healed different aspects of ourselves. During these moments, we all realized how connected we are in our pain. We also realized how much more deeply we connected as we healed ourselves together. The support we freely shared with each other was of a kind many of us never had experienced or known before. The support was truly unconditional. The QuantumPathic® Energy Method (QPEM) has changed the way I look at things.

I call the QuantumPathic® Energy Method (QPEM) the missing piece of the puzzle. Why? Because you can stop "telling your story" as you do with traditional therapy. You no longer have to look to someone else outside of yourself to help your "wanty needy" self.

You can step into your own power and allow yourself to heal. You learn to honor and listen to your body. It speaks volumes to you. As the Non-Emotional Observer (NEO), you can access tremendous amounts of information and use it to heal yourself. You can finally break free of the old ways of re-creating and re-creating what you don't "wanty needy". Now you start creating what you require, desire, and deserve. It's the key to setting yourself free!

I use the QPEM tools every day. They have assisted me both personally and professionally. As Sherry Anshara says…"Personal and professional are both the same." I no longer separate myself into these two categories or in any category or label that does not serve me. I choose wholeness. I love the freedom to be me!

CONNECTIONS

"Consciousness is the key to everything"

-Sherryism

Quantum Relationships

by Cindie Hubiak and Bob Wyndelts

What is a Quantum Relationship?

Our bodies knew we were a soul match before our minds protested. "It's too soon. Are you sure?" Society's admonitions made nary a ripple. After all, intelligence resides in the body, according to the QuantumPathic® Energy Method (QPEM). The mind is a tool, not intelligence. Bob's vision narrowed, as he surprisingly found that other women simply didn't exist. Realizing he felt safe, his defenses fell away. His body didn't demand immediate sexual activity. He experienced more of a desire to get to know Cindie.

Having studied the QuantumPathic® Energy Method (QPEM) for more than four years before meeting Bob, Cindie had learned how to live in her body by quieting her mind and listening to her heart. She had cleared much of the cellular memory that caused her to react in previous relationships. She could now pay attention to her old patterns of relationships, questioning whether she was reacting to emotions from the past or responding to a feeling in the present moment. Being with Bob felt like being home: contented, safe, and peaceful.

A quantum relationship connects mind, body, and soul. The intelligence of the body is followed, while the mind serves as an instrument, played and heard consciously, not with pre-recorded music from the past. Each moment creates newness, not a repetition of behaviors.

Early in our relationship, Bob sang a few lines from the song, "You Are My Sunshine", to Cindie. He didn't know that Cindie had unhappy memories of this song from her childhood. While the lyrics startled her at first, sending her back to an early age, she quickly became aware of being hijacked by an emotion from the past. She took a few deep breaths and found the ability to be present with the message of happiness Bob was sharing with her.

The newness created in this moment brought much joy, rather than disaster. If Cindie had reacted to emotions from the past, she would have started crying, confusing Bob, and causing him not to sing those lyrics again. The happiness created in that moment would have been replaced with emotions from the past, the type of minefield described by Bob later.

Cindie met Bob on a Grand Canyon hiking trip arranged by Peggy, a mutual friend. While familiar with his name, Cindie hadn't experienced a welcoming energy when she saw him across the room at a party several years prior at Peggy's home. Cindie knew Bob was one of eight people going on the hiking trip. When she arrived at Peggy's home to carpool and found Bob there, ready to ride along, she wasn't overly happy.

This changed the dynamics quite a bit, as Cindie had counted on a long drive filled with connected conversation and laughter. Now there was a stranger in the back seat with her, an individual whom she chose to approach with caution. She gathered her courage to ask Bob to move his car. "Peggy said I could park my car in the garage. Could you please move yours?" Cindie noted that he did so quickly, with just a momentary hesitation. "Well, that provides me some comfort that he's not a total jerk," Cindie thought. She shifted her original caution to more openness, knowing they would be sharing a four-hour car ride together.

To use the QuantumPathic® Energy Method language, seven years of dating provided Bob a clear sense of his desires and requirements for his soul match, along with some lingering needs/wants. Cindie was in the process of completing a 10-year relationship. Neither of our minds thought it was time for a new relationship. Obviously our bodies had different ideas.

During the 12 hours we spent hiking together in the Grand Canyon, Cindie asked Bob a plethora of questions. The conversations in the car and Bob's insistence that they sit next to each other at dinner caught her attention. She felt light-hearted in his presence, appreciating the masculine essence of his directness and focus.

Bob experienced a very deep, subtle connection with Cindie, so powerful that it quieted his mind on a regular basis. The first time was at Peggy's house, when Cindie asked him to move his car. His mind shouted, "But, I have a newer, nicer car." His body went into action, moving his car quickly and shutting down his mind. Bob enjoyed being near Cindie, as he could have a real conversation, feel comfortable, relaxed and at ease.

Sparks didn't fly for either of us. Instead, we experienced a continuous surge of energetic movement between our bodies. These feelings didn't grab either of us. They seeped through slowly and touched every single cell. Bob recalls feeling this way as we took a break part way down the Kaibab trail. We sat on the wooden slats leading up to an outhouse, eating apples and trail mix, feeling happy, talking, and in our own space.

Through our flowing conversation and active listening, Cindie discovered what Bob desired to provide his soul match. She knew Bob would be clear about what he would and wouldn't provide a woman. She found Bob's transparency in this area refreshing.

By taking classes and reading, Cindie knew that men are very thoughtful and honest when answering questions. She had to give Bob time to answer, unlike the fast back and forth conversations she experiences with girlfriends. Allowing him silence to contemplate his answers required a commitment to honoring him, which was made easy by her curiosity. His intelligence, life experiences and comfort while talking about sex, one of her favorite topics, allowed the 12-hour hike to pass quickly. By engaging in conversation this way, Cindie easily determined that what Bob desired to provide a woman matched her requirements and many of her desires.

Bob didn't think of Cindie as a potential partner during the hike. That came later. He experienced sheer joy from not guarding himself, a brand new experience. Cindie's self-assuredness, no agenda, and lack of judgment gave him the freedom to say whatever came to mind. Unlike other conversations, this one didn't have any minefields relating to old programs that had nothing to do with Bob. He felt viewed as an individual, not a representative of his gender. Again, this was a new experience for him. There was no nervousness, anxiety, or concern, only the feeling that Cindie let Bob be Bob.

Soon after the Grand Canyon hike, a colleague asked Bob if he knew how differently he was acting toward his relationship with Cindie. This person observed that Bob acted happier, more alive, light-hearted, energized, and focused. Bob was surprised to find that he didn't get distracted by his drive to acquire sex, even though he and Cindie hadn't had sex during this time. He also didn't compare Cindie to other people.

Bob wasn't aware of how much he had changed. Reflecting on his drastically different behavior, he realized that he listened to his body and overruled his mind. He told himself frequently, "Go with your gut. Your gut has never disappointed you."

Bob discovered that his body was so strong and powerful, that his mind didn't have a chance. He felt safe and trusted Cindie. He didn't step on any minefields with Cindie, she stayed committed to what she said, and she set him up for success. Bob realized he was enchanted with Cindie, an experience different from the past.

He completed relationships with other women, with one telling him, "What you have with Cindie is real. Throw out everything related to any other woman in your home." He followed her advice, finding items throughout his home that had been left there by other women and not noticed by him until now.

Soon after meeting Bob, Cindie suggested that Sherry Anshara energetically clear his home. He scheduled an appointment immediately, never having heard of this type of service. Afterward, Bob's home felt lighter and appeared brighter. The one family member who lived with him implemented Sherry Anshara's suggestions within a few days, despite skepticism at first. Bob now felt ready to explore a quantum relationship with Cindie.

Our Quantum Relationship Continues

Before meeting, we freed our Selves from much of the repressive conditioning due to societal, religious, and family expectations. We focused on becoming our authentic selves, clearing our bodies of patterns and energetic bands that no longer served us. We became more conscious and aware in each moment, providing the opportunity to hear the voice of our bodies over the voice of our minds.

We took different paths to bring these qualities into our lives. Before we met, both of us devoted time to our personal growth. We desired a relationship different than our parents, read a variety of books, and benefited from counseling experiences. Cindie also learned through international travel, meditation, business, and from the QuantumPathic® Energy Method (QPEM) starting in 2008. Before meeting Cindie, Bob learned through fatherhood, experiences as a university professor and small business owner, from seven years of dating, and from the QuantumPathic® Energy Method (QPEM) beginning when he met Cindie in 2012.

Excited to use the tools gathered from years of study, Cindie knew it was time to show up differently in this relationship. She understood the importance of integrating her feminine essence into life with Bob, not competing with him, and leading differently in this partnership. She made a commitment to not withdraw when an incident triggered emotions from the past and to speak up, making sure she was heard.

Bob knew it was time to change his independent way of making decisions, learn how to listen, and stop protecting himself. He knew Cindie was self-assured, didn't seek power from making decisions contrary to his, and could be trusted. He didn't yet have the skills required to be a partner in this relationship.

Three months into our relationship, we decided to buy a condo and live together. Cindie's apartment lease was over, we knew it didn't make sense to move into Bob's home, and it felt correct to buy a condo together. Our minds (and some "friends") questioned that quick choice. What transpired during the purchase and remodel of our sanctuary confirmed what our bodies knew: this was the correct approach.

Cindie was surprised one Friday afternoon to receive a text from Bob, "Can you look at a condo tonight?" Her first reaction was to say no, as she didn't know he was looking, and she experienced anger because he hadn't included her. "How dare he start this without me? How can we be partners if he doesn't talk with me about important matters like this?"

Being conscious allowed Cindie to take a deep breath and contemplate a response, different from her reaction. She knew her emotions were triggered, that she didn't feel in control, and didn't feel heard. She reminded herself of Bob's extensive experience in real estate, how he understood how busy she was at work, and discovered that she could allow Bob to lead in this area, freeing her time up for other activities.

The condo we saw matched our desires and felt like home. Our offer was made and accepted within a few days. Bob then took charge of another activity, fraught with arguments and minefields based on past experiences: a remodel. Bob knew his past history of doing what he wanted wouldn't work with Cindie. He continually reminded himself to slow down and engage her in decisions, even when he knew the correct answer.

Speaking up about her floor tile and furniture preferences was difficult for Cindie. She knew it was time to stop "living with" other people's decisions and to speak from her heart. It took every bit of courage she could find, especially when she was tired, to make herself heard. Early on, Bob told her he desired a woman who would go toe to toe with him. She reminded him of that during the purchase of dining rooms chairs that he thought were too expensive.

Without acquiescing on any item, we completed our remodel in a month, settling into living together with ease. We did what the QuantumPathic® Energy Method (QPEM) teaches: we dissolved most of our wanty/needy behaviors, thus eliminating our emotions previously based on control of others and situations. We became more conscious of our actions, identifying ones that arose from habit, and those we chose in the present moment.

We found this to be relatively easy to do in the beginning. Later on, we discovered some of our patterns became devious, hiding, and mixing with the other person's stuff, seeking survival. Fortunately, most of the time one of us remains non-emotional, supporting the other person to see the cellular memory that caused the emotion.

We knew the clarity of our requirements and desires in partnership allowed us to create a quantum relationship. Our souls matched, assisting in moving our relationship out of the traditional restrictions of duality and into a multi-dimensional world full of creativity and joy. Without wanty/needy behaviors, we changed our paradigms from the past, consciously allowing our bodies to guide us into this new relationship.

Through these early conversations about our requirements and desires, and understanding our remaining wanty/needy behaviors, we knew this was more than the typical sexual attraction each of us experienced in the past. We spent time alone, listening to our bodies. We spent time together, mostly being together instead of doing a variety of activities. This time allowed us to quiet our minds and hear our bodies, to stay in our bodies, not our minds.

Rather than go to movies, have dinner with friends, or attend charitable events, we consciously chose to minimize these activities. We spent most weekends hiking for hours. We would talk about what patterns were coming up and then hike in silence for some time, allowing us to contemplate our experiences.

We meditated together, starting each day in silence. Surprisingly, neither one of us played much music in our home, as the additional stimulation seemed too much for us with all we were processing. We rarely watch TV, so there was no adjustment in that area. When we drove to hiking spots, we would listen to or read material that provided us ideas to explore about relationship, sex, and consciousness.

We explored our past, seeing the patterns, and how our childhoods impacted our behaviors. We both kept lists of items to explore with Sherry Anshara during private sessions, cutting bands to people/behaviors and clearing behaviors that were about validation and judgment. We didn't talk much about our everyday lives. Instead, we explored our authentic Selves, uncovering layers that had been hidden for years. We knew our souls matched, bringing a closeness and ease in relationship never experienced before.

Benefits of a Quantum Relationship

Our quantum relationship allows us to project our individual and joint magnificence. A friend who hadn't seen us together commented, "You two radiate a palpable glow." We experience a freedom from expectation and attachment, combined with ecstatic living, improving our self-confidence, physical wellness, and resilience.

Friends keep asking if the honeymoon is over, if we are still in love with each other, noting that our relationship seems too good to be true. Each time we assure them that our closeness continues to deepen, our ecstasy increases, and we are free from anxiety about the relationship and expectations from the other.

When we stop at a vista during a favorite hike, arms around each other, people ask if we'd like our picture taken. They smile, seeing us holding hands as we leave the trailhead for our car. We laugh more often, moving past emotional experiences more quickly than before.

Our daily activities flow easier with greater presence and awareness. Work relationships are more fluid and natural, with our ability to bring light-hearted play into many moments. We connect more deeply with others and our Selves as our ability to feel compassion grows. We experience greater trust and unity through our love making.

Ways to Create a Quantum Relationship

Wordology

Words are powerful. Our bodies know what words ring true and correct. Learning to listen to our bodies when we speak, instead of allowing our minds to tell the same story, propelled us into our quantum relationship quickly.

The QuantumPathic® Energy Method (QPEM) teaches wordology as embedded vibration and meaning in the sound/sight of letters, words, and phrases. Did we mean "desire or want? Require or need? Correct or right? Assist or help?" Consciously choosing our words became part of our journey, allowing us to understand and clearly communicate. We still laugh at ourselves when we revert to the use of emotionally charged words.

Desiring a quality or object doesn't include an emotional context, while wanting is an emotion based in control. Have you ever said, "If I just had _______, everything would be all right," or "I'd be happy if ________"? These statements express wants, not desires, and contain a belief that someone or something has control over you.

Desire, on the other hand, is a non-emotional feeling. This probably sounds counter-intuitive. It did to us in the beginning. As Sherry Anshara explains earlier in the book, all feelings are non-emotional. As we clear our cellular memories, we discover that emotions disappear from our relationship and our lives, leaving only room for feelings like desire. We can desire anything, a new car, relationship of our dreams, or winning the lottery, while retaining a state of happiness, even if our desires are not fulfilled. The QuantumPathic® Energy Method (QPEM) teaches the creation of joy from the inside, freeing us from the belief that our happiness comes from others, instead of our Selves.

For example, consider these statements. "I want you to hold me. I need you," versus "I feel a desire for closeness. Would you be willing to hold me now?" How did your body respond to each of these requests? Which one feels correct, more powerful?

In the beginning of our relationship, Cindie often wanted Bob to hold her, give her a kiss or rub her neck. If Bob said no or not now, she would experience her throat tightening, her tummy clenching, and her heart closing down. Processing these experiences using the QuantumPathic® Energy Method (QPEM), Cindie realized her body was experiencing emotions of rejection from the past, a need for validation from Bob and/or a lack of love for her Self. She was wanting, not desiring. She came from a place of emotions from the past, not strength in the present.

As Cindie changed her language, cleared the past, and became more aware, she knew that no one, including Bob, can validate her. That the rejection she experienced in the past is not part of her relationship with Bob. She realized that depending on anyone or anything for her well-being and happiness didn't bring her joy.

This didn't stop Cindie from enjoying a physical closeness and connection with Bob. Instead, she found the words 'desire' and 'require' started to resonate within her body. She feels strong, powerful, and clear when she uses these words. She actually stands up taller and feels her heart open wider. She began to acquire a deeper understanding of how the words she uses impacts her Self and all her relationships.

If Bob indicates he is in the middle of a project and will hug her later, Cindie doesn't take this personally. She remains happy and able to enjoy other activities until Bob is ready to take a break. She realizes now that she attempted to control Bob by using words like 'want' and 'need', almost like commanding him to give her a hug. She recalls feeling sick to her stomach and noticing that her shoulders slumped when she used these words. She realized she was manipulating the situation by appealing to his emotions, not giving him a chance to say no. This takes away his freedom.

We enjoy fulfilling each other's desires and the feeling of freedom that comes with it. By releasing control of the other person, we come from a place of strength. Our bodies feel more powerful when we use words that resonate with them.

As Bob listens to Cindie express a desire for physical connection, he knows he can make a choice without emotional consequences. He can determine quickly if an immediate connection with Cindie supports their relationship or if it's wiser to complete his activity, connecting with her as soon as he can be completely present.

Our bodies didn't resonate with all the QuantumPathic® Energy Method (QPEM) wordology in the beginning. It didn't feel natural, as we still had emotional baggage from the past, tying us to words that kept us weak. It took both of us time to realize the power of discerning 'desires' and 'requirements' in our lives instead of 'wants' or 'needs'. The chronic state of neediness implies hardship, destitution, and poorness, conditions that can continue. 'Require' is a more powerful word and shows a clarity of purpose that rings true to us now.

As we look back on how Bob made a choice to be in a quantum relationship with Cindie, he discovered that he required a fit, attractive, intelligent, confident woman whom he found sexually compatible. Previously he wanted to have sex with beautiful women. Cindie knew the next man in her life must provide the opportunity to expand her spirituality through their sexual relationship, be financially stable, and support the empowerment of women. In the past, she needed a man who would put his career behind hers. We both required a polarity of the masculine and feminine, with a solid integration of both energies in our partner.

Bob desired a woman who shared his humble beginnings. Cindie desired a man who values sustainable living and honors the planet. We knew these qualities were not required of our soul match, nor did these desires come from a place of want or need.

A requirement is not optional. Cindie's requirement regarding Bob's financial stability was not negotiable. She didn't need Bob's money. She did require him to be successful enough to not require her money. If Cindie viewed her Self as needing Bob to be financially stable, she would be giving away her power to Bob.

The energy of the word 'need' impacts the body and creates a dependency that allows control and manipulation. While using the word 'require' felt demanding and rigid in the beginning, we soon realized how free it allowed our bodies to feel and how much more joy we could experience.

Using the word 'correct', instead of 'right', provides clarity of meaning without judgment. As Bob prepared to be cross-examined in a lawsuit related to a business transaction, Cindie observed his strong emotions when talking about the case.

"He's wrong and I'm right!" said Bob.

When Cindie asked Bob about this, he stopped, took a deep breath, and realized the other party held the same opinion. Because of his understanding of the QuantumPathic® Energy Method (QPEM) wordology, Bob began to see that his view of the case came from his emotions. After a few more minutes of conversation with Cindie, Bob discarded the emotional word 'right', replacing it with the word 'correct'.

Changing his view from 'right' to 'correct' meant Bob shifted his perspective from an emotional state to one focused on the facts. He knew there were still lingering emotions related to the lawsuit, though, so he was not fully prepared to testify.

He asked Cindie for her help. She asked if he was requesting 'help' or 'assistance'. As he checked in with his body, his body felt weaker when he considered the word 'help'. It felt like he gave up his power and wasn't capable of handling the situation. His body responded differently when he used the word 'assist'. He felt a surge of strength, stood straighter, and felt ready to handle any situation that came his way. He would be on the witness stand, no one else, so he changed his request.

With Cindie's coaching, Bob moved from 'needing help' to 'desiring assistance'. He retained responsibility for the preparation of his testimony. After about two hours of hiking, Bob had released all the emotional stories from this experience and shared just the facts with Cindie.

Bob retained his power and ability to communicate clearly as a result of changing his wordology and dissolving his emotions. In court, Bob remained the non-emotional observer, providing testimony valuable for the judge. The other party exhibited disrespectful emotional behavior, causing the judge to evict him from the court room. Several months later, the judge ruled entirely in Bob's favor.

Validate Your Self

We both grew up in environments where thoughts and anxieties like "What will the neighbors think?" controlled our parents' behavior. As children, we learned to change our behaviors to align with the expectations of others, not the desires of our authentic Selves.

Bob's childhood was greatly influenced by the Catholic Church. It appeared to Bob that the Church attempted to make him feel like a loser by instilling guilt, an emotion that doesn't serve him. Cindie grew up not trusting men, carrying this belief into her adult life. Both of our childhoods led us to believe we weren't good enough, causing us to doubt our Selves and our value, no matter the extent of our achievements.

Through a variety of efforts, including the QuantumPathic® Energy Method (QPEM), we disposed of the need for validation from external sources and learned to validate our Selves. Now Cindie doesn't require validation from Bob and thus, doesn't give her power away to him. Bob knows his authentic self, therefore not requiring validation from Cindie. Admonitions inundated us, as others questioned our sanity in committing to each other after about three weeks from meeting each other in the Grand Canyon. Again, we possessed the confidence and clarity to not require validation from others. Our bodies knew.

The QuantumPathic® Energy Method (QPEM) assists us in releasing the past from our cellular memory where it no longer serves us. It guides us to dissolve limiting belief systems, such as needing validation from other people and institutions such as religious organizations. The QuantumPathic® Energy Method

(QPEM) clears cellular memories in the body and brain, where we store emotional experiences. Sherry Anshara describes how this is done earlier in the book. Unhealthy memories present in the body cause disease and discomfort, in addition to causing us to act in unconscious ways.

Disposition of Emotional Baggage

We enjoy calling the disposition of emotional baggage the recognition and owning of our own stuff. Specifically, this means learning how to discern Bob's stuff, Cindie's stuff, and the most difficult of all, our stuff. We discovered this process required a desire and focused discipline to rid our bodies of memories and/or belief systems that no longer serve us. We learned to recognize our emotional baggage from prior relationships. We remembered patterns and behaviors that created distance and fear, reducing the intimacy we sought.

Early in our relationship, Cindie experienced hurt when Bob answered a question on a magazine quiz, indicating Cindie was more overweight than he. Cindie's immediate reaction was to withdraw by abruptly ending our conversation. Cindie knew she withdrew when she was afraid. She knew her body caused her to withdraw unconsciously to avoid emotional pain. She'd already owned this behavior as her stuff and had committed to eliminating it when she met Bob. In that moment, she became aware of her reaction, took a deep breath to get into her body, and began dissipating the stress she felt.

She let Bob know she wanted to withdraw. She instinctively curled into a fetal position on the couch, forcing herself to stay in conversation with Bob. Knowing Cindie's desire to dissolve this pattern, Bob started asking her questions. "Let me assist you in staying in the conversation and digging deep. Where is the pain, Cindie?"

"My throat is closed, my tummy is tied up in knots, and my shoulders are stiff as a board. This is really difficult. I don't want to talk about it."

"You can do this. You frequently tell me you're committed to showing up differently in our relationship by letting go of past behaviors. You know I love your body and how you look. Why do you think you reacted so strongly?"

"You didn't say you loved my body. You compared me to Society's view of women. You know I'm happy with my body and my weight. You, you, you, you're mean," Cindie cried out through her tears.

At this point, it was all Bob could do not to react and become emotional. He took some deep breaths, contemplating his behavior and how he had compared Cindie to other women. His old emotions related to 'not doing anything right' were ready to pounce on Cindie. With considerable effort, he stayed focused on Cindie.

"Comparing you to other women and how Society views women is mean, Cindie, and I apologize for that. Stay with me, and let's go deeper. You are typically confident and self-assured. What's happening?

Cindie's aha moment came quickly. Her body relaxed, her throat opened, she kept breathing deeply. "I think this is getting clear. I'm seeking your validation. I love you. You've dated a lot of women, and I'm not interested in losing weight. From childhood, I've been taught to please others, to do what they wanted me to do, and not validate my Self. People have gotten angry with me and left me in the past when I didn't please them." She let out a big sigh.

"Awesome! Sounds like you got it. This makes a lot of sense from what you've told me."

"It does. Thank you for your patience and guidance through this process. I can see how I could have asked you questions to better understand your answer, avoiding this painful situation. I couldn't do it, though. The emotional trigger I've worked on for years to release was still there. This experience has given me new skills, plus I have a session with Sherry Anshara next week and can further delve into this need for validation."

Cindie continued with a playful tone, "Now let's look at your stuff. You did a magnificent job of staying non-emotional. Thank you. Tell me why you saw me as overweight and not you."

As we talked about this part of our conversation, Bob realized he used a societal definition of appearance. He had viewed the question about his weight and Cindie's weight based on Society's norms, not his own. His experience showed that Society allows men to be heavier than women, causing him to say Cindie is overweight.

"I apologize, Cindie, for my past view of women's bodies that were based on what the popular press tells us is overweight. I can see why that concerned you, and I commit to being careful about forming my own opinions, not blindly following Society's."

In medical terms, we are not overweight. What started as an innocent, fun quiz, deteriorated into an emotional situation that could have resulted in us avoiding conversations, making decisions not in our best interests, and withdrawing. Instead, Bob stayed non-emotional and coached Cindie through her stuff, later allowing her to coach him through his. This conversation brought us closer together, with a greater understanding of how we could each do something differently in the future.

To share another example, Bob began to notice a need to control the conversation, to be right, to be heard, and not to listen to Cindie. He now realizes this behavior protected him from being criticized, a common experience he had as a child and in previous relationships.

One afternoon, Cindie angrily said to Bob, "You never date me." Cindie recited several emotional stories to show why she believed this to be true. Instead of responding to Cindie's storm as the non-emotional observer and allowing her emotions to flow around him, Bob reacted to Cindie emotionally. He started defending himself, which only served to escalate the emotionality of the situation. After several heated exchanges, Bob requested a Time Out.

During the Time Out, the emotion drained away to where we became the non-emotional observers of our Selves. We became 'of it, not in it.' To do this, Bob pictures the earth as the size of a baseball, with him looking at it from a distance. Cindie pictures her Self floating above the action, watching and observing. From this space, Cindie reflected on all Bob did, rather than what he didn't do. She saw how she made up non-factual stories. Bob remembered that no one can admonish him without his permission. He knew he wasn't lazy and did all he could to support Cindie.

As we talked about what happened, we saw several emotional triggers that arose. Cindie's 'men don't support me' trigger connected with Bob's 'I can never do enough' trigger. Bob understood his triggers of not feeling adequate and being admonished.

This provided us with an outstanding example of what can happen when our stuff collides. Both of us reacted emotionally and neither of us was able to assist the other. We committed to supporting the one in the most emotional pain whenever possible, providing us with the non-emotional experience of the magazine quiz instead of the 'you don't date me' emotional minefield.

Be Present

In order for us to create a quantum relationship, we learned the importance of talking without distractions and being completely present with the other. This requires considerable practice, more for Bob than Cindie. Living in the 'always on' world with his CPA practice and wanting to avoid difficult topics in personal relationships, Bob used distraction to tune out what he didn't want to hear. He would redirect conversations with a story from the past or talk about something in his field of vision. He became a master at avoiding what he didn't want to talk about.

With constant diligence and friendly reminders from Cindie, Bob learned how to focus on our conversation, no matter the irrelevant thoughts that intruded or what he saw in the room. He learned to look at Cindie more frequently, and she learned to guide him back into the present. Cindie also learned how to speak more succinctly, providing Bob headlines and not all the details.

Additionally, after an intense work day, something as simple as 15 minutes of yoga increases our capacity to focus, sheds the energy from the day, and allows us to experience a more connected evening together. We keep our yoga practice simple. Bob typically leads with two sun salutations, twists, and an inversion. The twists are either seated or prone, designed to "ring out" our inner organs. Our inversion can be as simple as legs up the wall. While this practice is not specifically designed for couples, it connects us in a nourishing way in the present moment.

Full Transparency

We committed to full transparency to expand our quantum relationship. We share really petty thoughts and not so petty thoughts with each other. We call this sharing 'True Confessions'. We often 'confess' during a hike, providing an environment to share intimate information that creates feelings of vulnerability at first, and later, feelings of lightness.

These confessions can be as seemingly simple as, "You eat more food than I do, yet I pay for half the food," or "I drive my car everywhere, and you don't pay for any gas." These True Confessions give us big laughs, and we frequently discard them. Bringing these apparently petty thoughts to the other supports the awareness of our thoughts. We talk about our confessions until resolved. We make sure we don't stuff them, and therefore don't create an inventory of resentment.

Other True Confessions seem more difficult to share. Cindie became aware of a thought about a give/get scenario with Bob, "If he would buy dinner tonight, I will make sure he gets sex." Cindie wondered why this occurred as it wasn't part of her relationship with Bob.

She decided to 'confess' it to Bob, keeping their commitment to full transparency. Bob smiled in recognition of this old belief of his, and we laughed at how this belief system still endured in a relationship where sex and money are abundant. Cindie felt lighter, knowing she expressed this thought. Her conversation with Bob allowed her to further dissolve this old, engrained belief system.

Summary

Continuing to create a quantum relationship requires dedication, commitment, and presence. Fortunately, we find old patterns repeating themselves less and less over time. What once seemed difficult has now become a way of life, magnificently rewarding us with the experiences of sustainable joy.

Quantum Sex

by Cindie Hubiak and Bob Wyndelts

What is Quantum Sex?

Just saying 'quantum sex' sounds wondrous. AND IT IS. Quantum sex provides us with pleasure beyond imagination, deep connection, and travels without a passport. As we listen to our bodies, we expand and extend our orgasms, with clothes on or off. As we become completely present with each other, our intimacy increases. Quantum sex allows our bodies to take us places our minds cannot imagine.

We enjoy backpacking into the Superstition Mountains near Phoenix, Arizona. The wild beauty of this infamous place delights our senses. It quiets our minds, allowing us to more easily listen to our bodies.

One chilly spring morning, with our tent put away, water filtered, and ready to hike, we stopped to share words of appreciation. Facing each other, holding hands, we found our bodies moving in orgasmic bliss. Clothes on, barely touching, completely in the moment. This is just one example of quantum sex.

During our initial conversations about sex, Cindie described her desire for a sacred sexual journey, one she defined as connecting to her Self, a partner, and the multi-verse. Bob knew such a relationship was possible, had been searching for one, and didn't know much more.

Together we discovered that quantum sex is not a set of specific techniques. It's not a cookie cutter process. Instead, it's a unique way of being for each individual. It's living life with authenticity, with awareness of our body, and using our mind as a tool.

Experiencing quantum sex is possible through conscious clearing of emotional programs related to life and those specifically related to sex. Using the QuantumPathic® Energy Method (QPEM), we began getting out of our heads and into our bodies.

Quantum sex is connection without baggage, without emotional neediness. It is created in each moment as a new experience. Quantum sex fills us with joy and radiance that spills into all aspects of our lives.

Benefits of Quantum Sex

For Bob, quantum sex increases his energy, clarity, and focus. All aspects of Bob's life now vibrate at a different, more enjoyable resonance. After meeting Cindie, he quickly realized that non-quantum sex no longer satisfied him. While his physical needs could be satisfied by non-quantum sex, it resulted in exhaustion, listlessness, and diffusion. His body told him there was more to sex than satisfying his physical needs.

For Cindie, quantum sex fulfills her quest for allness. It allows her to be intimate and connected with her Self, with Bob, and with the multi-verse. Quantum sex allows her to explore her femininity, receive Bob's gifts, and take him along for rides he can't go on alone.

Two of Cindie's emotional programs related to sex have interfered with us experiencing quantum sex more frequently. Sometimes Cindie runs a sacrifice program and a 'men don't show up for her' program. In conversation with other women, Cindie finds she's not alone. Perhaps you recognize this pattern and are ready to clear it also.

One day, Cindie became angry with Bob because she perceived he wasn't present during their love making. His eyes had closed more frequently and he didn't respond to her signals. She experienced a disconnection from him and decided to get even by not having any orgasms. She didn't want him to experience the satisfaction of knowing he provided her pleasure.

Epitomizing the sacrifice program, Cindie's emotional neediness prevented her from enjoying her Self. She sabotaged her pleasure by validating her belief that men don't show up for her. Recognizing this dysfunctional behavior, Cindie talked with Bob about it and worked with the QuantumPathic® Energy Method (QPEM) to clear these emotions.

Through conversation with Bob, Cindie discovered ways she can communicate more clearly, even in the 'heat of the moment'. Cindie committed to expressing her desires directly, no matter how difficult. Bob agreed to support Cindie by encouraging her to convey her experiences.

Within the last month, Cindie began to understand the importance of Bob periodically moving into his own sexual experience. Knowing she can facilitate Bob's pleasure and potential emotional healing of his own, provides Cindie with a new way to experience what previously had been Bob's disconnection from her. With this shift, she feels joy from supporting Bob in a very unique way.

Working with the QuantumPathic® Energy Method (QPEM), Cindie realized she sacrifices her pleasure and seeks to punish Bob in order to validate her childhood program that men don't show up for her. As Cindie goes back to those times, she clears these emotions, knowing she is the only one who can validate her Self. She sees the past in different ways, supporting a new way of life where men show up for her.

Getting Started

In this section, we provide steps to guide your journey of lasting ecstatic pleasure, along with examples and suggestions. You can begin to experience quantum sex at any point in your relationship. While we started our practice almost from the beginning, we believe this journey can be made by couples at any point in their time together.

Wherever you are in your relationship, begin by opening or expanding your dialogue about sex. Find a safe space in which to share, establishing ground rules like using a talking stick to allow the person holding an object to speak without interruption. Set a timer to allow both of you to share. Observe what comes up for you and use the QuantumPathic® Energy Method (QPEM) or other resources to clear what we affectionately call "your stuff".

We didn't start out having quantum sex. When we met in 2012, we began our relationship by talking for five weeks about sex (and a few other items) before our first sexual intercourse. This seemed like an eternity for us and is not required.

For us, our bodies suggested we use this time as an investment in our future. Our bodies knew the more we could share our desires and concerns, and the more we could process past emotions, the more extraordinary sexual experiences we could create.

Our conversations about sex continue to this day, allowing us to deepen our connection and pleasure. As we share what our bodies feel and any emotions that arise both during sex and after, we find buried experiences that require healing and belief systems that no longer serve us. We also discover new ways to listen to our bodies and support each other to enjoy more ecstasy.

One day this week after making love, Cindie shared with Bob that she didn't feel much pleasure and experienced him being focused on his sensations at the exclusion of hers. She communicated this in a non-judgmental way, making it clear to Bob that this wasn't his fault. As we talked, Bob stayed non-emotional, trusting that Cindie wasn't accusing him of not being good enough, a past belief that no longer serves him.

This situation is similar to the one described earlier when Cindie experienced a disconnection from Bob. The repetition of this experience illustrates how our minds can be devious, disguising emotions in different ways. We observed the importance of staying non-emotional and supporting each other to release old patterns during our conversation.

We laughed at how Cindie's conniving mind continues to bring up emotional programs related to pleasing Bob at the expense of her well-being, an inability to express her desires when she becomes upset, and her fear associated with men not showing up for her.

Bob explored situations that might cause him to disconnect from Cindie to focus on his own pleasure. He considered times when he experienced emasculation and a long-held belief that women take advantage of him.

All of these programs (and several others) get in our way of enjoying quantum sex, as our minds attempt to run our lives from the past. Our conversations increase awareness of our thoughts, allowing us to discard unhealthy ones before we become emotional. We identify beliefs that no longer serve us and clear them with the assistance of the QuantumPathic® Energy Method (QPEM).

While it may seem that we don't value our minds, we do, when we use them in beneficial ways. One way our minds serve us is by studying conscious loving and tantric energy practices. From the beginning of our relationship, Cindie shared information with Bob from classes and teachers she had discovered. We continue to work with Sherry Anshara to dissolve belief systems and clear ancient history. We read books suggested by Jivana Kennedy, including ones by David Deida, Diana Richardson, Michael Richardson, and Barry Long. We are now gaining knowledge from the playful and wise Layla Martin.

We invite you to do what we do: practice and have fun! We practice listening to our bodies, sharing what our minds shout loudly and softly, no matter how unpleasant, and slow down our love making to really feel the sensations. By doing this, we create an expansion of our quantum relationship into the wondrous, surprising, delightful journey of quantum sex.

Creating Quantum Sex

Prioritize and Schedule Time Together

We started our quest for quantum sex by retraining Bob's mind from an attitude of starvation and lack to a place of abundance. It took almost a year for his mind to accept what his body already knew: sex is almost always available with Cindie.

Before he met Cindie, Bob was virtually always starved for sex. Except for the first few hours after non-quantum sex, he devoted much of his energy to acquiring additional sex. He ran a give/get program, where he would take a woman to dinner in exchange for sex or assist her with a home project, expecting sex as a reward. This was a conscious program he found typically existing as an unspoken agreement between men and women.

All that changed when Bob met Cindie, as this give/get program could not exist as part of a quantum sex relationship. Cindie suggested that time be scheduled for sex, prioritizing intimacy. She also made a commitment to be available to Bob as much as possible when he requested sex.

In the beginning, it seemed to Cindie that Bob might never leave his lack program. Most of the time, Cindie enjoyed the love making, believing Bob would shift into a place where he wasn't so needy. When she wasn't able to provide sex for him, she clearly explained the reason, requested his understanding, and made sure a time was set in the near future for love making.

With Cindie's commitment to sexual activity and follow-through, and using the QuantumPathic® Energy Method (QPEM), Bob cleared his lack program and now knows that sex with Cindie is abundant. Instead of completing a chore or buying Cindie flowers as payment for sex, Bob has moved into a space where he enjoys providing for Cindie solely for the resulting feeling of joy. He knows that caring for Cindie supports the partnership and he willingly offers assistance to Cindie.

For the first time in Bob's life, he is not starved for sex. He no longer devotes much of his energy to the acquisition of sex. Instead, this energy is available for his use in each moment. Bob dissolved the give/get program that had been running his life, allowing him to experience more pleasure and delight in relationship than he imagined.

There are times when Cindie desires sex and Bob isn't able to provide it. During these times, she typically can take the focus off her Self and move into compassion for Bob. In her heart, she knows he would support her if possible. She knows he's not punishing her or withholding his connection from her. She finds other ways to connect with him and satisfy her desires, including setting a date with him for sex.

Last night we both desired sex and made up stories that prevented us from enjoying love making. Bob told Cindie he was tired and sleepy, so she assumed he wouldn't be interested in sex. After getting into bed, Bob felt a desire to connect with Cindie sexually and thought she wouldn't be interested because of his perception of a comment she made earlier in the day.

Bob's mind ran an old program related to his fear of rejection and not being validated by a woman. Because he still experiences some emotions involving not being good enough, Bob went to sleep without letting Cindie know he desired sex.

We talked about this situation the next morning, amused by the cleverness of the mind. If Bob had followed his body's desire and not listened to his mind, we probably would have enjoyed quantum sex. We both made new commitments to listen to our bodies and express our desires.

Be Present – No Fantasizing

From the beginning of our relationship, we committed to listening to our bodies. Our bodies know what to do and provide clarity when we listen to them. Our minds focus on baggage from the past, emotions, and the future. Our bodies carry no such burden. Listening to our bodies requires us to live in the present moment.

With other lovers, our minds fantasized during sex, moving us out of our bodies and out of the present moment. Often Cindie would visualize a scene from a book she had read or think about her to do list, while Bob fantasized about being with someone else or a woman he created in his mind.

Fantasizing took us to another place in time. It disconnected us from our partner, from our bodies, and the present moment. This resulted in an activity more like mutual masturbation. Why choose that, when we can choose the pleasure of quantum sex?

During our initial conversations about sex, we committed to eliminating fantasies. As Bob puts it, "No more pump and squirt sex". We agreed to support each other no matter what emotions arise and to encourage each other to stay present, no matter how much we want to go somewhere else.

As described more in the next section, Cindie experiences a wide range of feelings and emotions during sex. Rather than fantasize to avoid the painful emotions, Cindie stays present with each one, allowing her to move past blockages that prevent her from experiencing greater and greater ecstasy.

Eliminating fantasies requires Bob to open his heart and find the courage to stay with the entire range of Cindie's emotions and feelings. He doesn't hide behind fantasies any more, knowing his presence is required to support Cindie. He also experiences enhanced pleasure when he stays in his body.

Being present creates a spiritual connection and integration with each other. Sex is no longer mechanical and performance-oriented. It is a delicious journey of discovery, clearing past patterns, and supporting each other to heal sexual and non-sexual wounds.

Healing – Physically

As we became more present during our love making, we discovered a sensitivity and healing assistance contained within the head of Bob's penis. We had read about this, so were familiar with the concept of how a man's penis can assist a woman's vagina to heal. While it sounded weird, we proceeded with curiosity and discovered it to be the truth!

Lately we hear the term 'de-armoring of the vagina' being used to describe this experience. This term makes sense to us, as it illustrates how vaginas build up protection from a variety of traumas. As this armor is removed with loving connection, the vagina opens, becomes softer, and more able to experience pleasure.

Bob physically feels through his penis when healing is desired. He describes Cindie's vagina grabbing his penis, insisting that he stay in a specific spot. Other times his penis senses an increase in energy, pulling him toward an exact location. Often this area feels unexplored, as if it has not been penetrated recently or it feels hard, almost hurting his penis.

Bob allows the head of his penis to stay still on these spots until he feels a softening in Cindie's vagina. Keeping his penis on this spot takes focus and concentration. Bob's penis can feel excessive heat, pain, and even Cindie's fear, when on one of these spots. His mind attempts to get him to move, to shift back to friction sex. His mind might taunt, "If you don't move, you'll get soft," or "You will never get off by being still." Bob's body knows better, allowing him to dismiss his mind's antics and support Cindie's healing with his presence.

Bob finds talking to Cindie assists him to stay in his body and ignore his mind. He shares what he feels, whether it be a hardness or Cindie's fear. He asks her questions, holds her, and encourages her to express her Self through crying, screaming, kicking, or other methods to release whatever is stored in her body.

A few times there has been a searing pain that forces Cindie to be aware of the exact spot in her vagina that requires healing. This surprises her, as one minute she is in ecstasy, the next in pain. Other times, she's not aware of the hard spot Bob feels in her vagina. She doesn't consciously guide Bob to specific spots or experience emotions before he feels a spot.

As Bob talks with her, Cindie stays focused on the location until the pain or emotions dissipate. Bob's voice and encouragement support Cindie staying in her body and not escaping through her mind. No matter how painful, she knows that staying with the experience will provide her healing and comfort.

Cindie doesn't know what may have caused a spot to require healing. Because she feels safe with Bob and stays in her body, she can fully release these old wounds. At this time, we haven't found Bob requiring specific physical healing. We understand that men also store trauma in their bodies, so we believe similar techniques can be used to support a man in his physical healing.

Healing – Emotionally

Just as physical healing is required for quantum sex, emotional healing is also required. We began by examining barriers to fully experiencing pleasure and shining a light on our emotional baggage that repeated itself in other relationships, intimate and non-intimate.

Through our conversations, we identified some of our dysfunctional patterns. We found others along the way through classes with Sherry Anshara, journaling, and observing recurring behaviors that didn't serve us.

One night, Cindie started listing what Bob didn't do, justifying her unhealthy belief that men didn't support her. "You forgot to pick up the dry cleaning, didn't ask about my big meeting, and you didn't want sex when I initiated it yesterday," she whined.

Often Bob's unhealthy belief that he's not good enough would kick in, causing him to emotionally engage with Cindie by justifying his actions and blaming her. This evening he broke that pattern! "I apologize, Cindie. I'll pick up the dry cleaning tomorrow and ask that you remind me about big events in your day." Remaining non-emotional, Bob then asked, "I didn't know you initiated sex last night. You know it's pretty rare when I'm not interested. Could you be finding a way to justify men not supporting you?"

Cindie took a deep breath, causing her to move into her body and out of her mind. With Bob staying non-emotional and compassionate, she had a better opportunity to shift out of the victim program and clear yet another layer of emotions related to men not supporting her. She then listed several activities Bob does to support her, affirming his assistance, and strengthening her new belief that men show up for her.

As we wrote this chapter, Bob realized that before meeting Cindie, he used sex for validation, an emotional need of his. He had to have sex with a woman within a few dates in order to continue the relationship, validating his worthiness. With Cindie, he had no timeline for their first sexual encounter. Unknowingly, Bob had moved into his body and out of his head.

Bob's body knew sex with Cindie would happen at a time that was perfect for this new type of relationship. His body was in charge of the timing, overruling his mind's history of viewing women as sexual opportunities.

As we shift our focus from our minds to our hearts, clearing our emotional baggage becomes easier. We trust each other to identify belief systems that no longer serve us. This results in less emotionality during sex, freeing up our bodies to feel pleasure and not revisit the pains from the past.

Communication from the Heart

Quantum sex expands communication as we listen to our bodies. Our ability to use non-verbal communication increases as we move out of our heads. Without old thought patterns that used to be repeated in our minds, we create newness in each moment.

To experience quantum sex, we often begin our love making with rituals that assist us in moving from our heads into our bodies. We breathe deeply, gaze into each other's eyes, and concentrate on the energy movement between us. We sit across from each other, allowing each person to share their desires for our time together and any concerns. We express our appreciation for each other in ways that connect us.

As we entrain, our bodies begin to vibrate at the identical frequency such that we become a single energetic entity. This amplifies the resonance of our sexual experience. Our eyes generally remain open and focused on each other as we continue our love making, further supporting our entrainment and our presence in that moment.

At some point after our love making, we talk about our experiences, sharing what we enjoyed, any emotions that arose, and our appreciation for the other. This ongoing commitment to communication means we process anything that might prohibit us from the joys of quantum sex and keeps us out of our heads and in our bodies.

Multiple Energetic Orgasms

"You want me to do what?" exclaimed Bob the first time Cindie talked about men experiencing orgasms without ejaculation. The concept was unfathomable to him. Cindie had read about and witnessed how ejaculation depleted a man's body and spirit. Not having experienced a man having an orgasm without ejaculation, she was ready to support Bob in obtaining a new skill, opening up unknown territory for exploration.

Cindie explained her understanding of how men could move energy out of their genitals into other parts of their bodies. This allows men to engage in sex for a much longer time and experience increased pleasure. Bob read *Tantric Sex for Men* by the Richardsons, providing him with enough explanation to get started.

It took us close to a year of fun practice before Bob could reliably not ejaculate and accumulate energy to experience multiple orgasms during a single love making session without ejaculating. Now he can easily vary his speed, extend our love making time, and allow energy to move from his genitals throughout his entire body in orgasmic waves.

This accumulation of energy supports a more present, energetic, and satisfying life for Bob. Even his work flows more smoothly and he consistently feels a more sustainable joy. Now, the goal of ejaculation has become unimaginable. Ejaculation does occur. It occurs when we choose, based on what our bodies tell us. Bob challenges men to embrace the steep learning curve, as the payoff is magnificent. "Every aspect of your life will take a quantum leap," Bob observes.

For Cindie, Bob's ability to extend our love making allows her to experience more pleasure and deeper orgasms. She experiences Bob's blissful state, appreciating his ability to feel so deeply. With these feelings, we connect through quantum sex with our Selves, each other, and the multi-verse.

Summary

As we continue to explore quantum sex, our hearts connect and our souls match. We stay completely present, move energy between us in delicious ways, and clear emotions that do not serve us. May you experience joy, intimacy, and expansion as you explore quantum relationships and quantum sex.

MORE INFORMATION

"Listen to your body.
It holds all the answers.

Listen only to your brain,
and all you hear are the stories."

-Sherryism

All Your Answers are in the Questions…

It's how you ask the questions
that give you the Truth instead of what's true.

Sherry Anshara's Unusual Journey: An Amazing Awakening

by Sherry Anshara

To say "my life was normal" is an understatement. At three years old, in a Catholic family living in Detroit, Michigan, I said to my mother…"Remember when I was Jewish and lived in New York?" Of course she had no idea what I was talking about. At the time I didn't know how to explain it to her, and the words "Jewish" and "New York" were not part of my family's regular vocabulary. I am sure my mother didn't know what to think about it. In her idea, it was best to just ignore me.

When I was little, my father had some antique eye wash glasses. I would sit underneath our dining room table, with a small table set covered with my mother's doilies, and pretend with these glasses that I was having a "cocktail party" with my friends. Memories from New York. Playing tea parties just didn't do it for me!!! At the time, cocktails were also not a part of my family's conversation. Again, Mother's idea was that it was best to ignore me.

There were times I would tell Mother about the lights around the statue of Mary and talk about the lights I saw around certain people. She would tell me I was "not seeing" them and that my eyes were playing tricks on me. Yet I knew I was seeing lights. Of course, at the time I didn't know it was the natural aura, the electro-magnetic field that surrounds everything. My mother's idea was that it was best to continue to ignore me. My mother would smile and just ignore what she felt was my wild imagination. What else could she think? Lights around people – how funny is that!

At three, I was put in an oxygen tent in the hospital, listening to my father telling my mother that I would be okay. I was sitting up in this hospital crib, Buddha style, thinking to my Self…"No, I won't be okay. I really don't want to be here." At the time, I didn't fully comprehend that I didn't want to be here on Earth. Later in my life, in a time continuum session, I remembered a Being, other than my parents or the hospital staff, being in the room with me. At that moment, I felt very protected. Although I did not share this with my parents because saying anything would have been pointless.

I got through these experiences. I was bothered with bronchitis up through my late 30's. In terms of Consciousness, the difficulties in the respiratory system represent emotional issues, not being able to breathe into life. This makes sense. How could I breathe into life when no one knew what I was talking about?

Many would look at this picture and think what a perfect picture of a child with the perfect Santa Claus. Here I am at five years old, and if you look closely, I was not "buying" any of it. I am looking directly into the Santa's eyes with my hand on my hip…and the expression on my face says it all. What am I doing here? Stop with the fairy tales and let's get down to business. Oh well, another time then!

Throughout my life, I have had many experiences — telepathic, empathic, visitations, channeling — that it is almost hard for me to believe that I actually lived from an outward perspective of a normal life. How amazing is the body, the soul, the spirit, and the divine mind that it can live these multi-dimensional experiences without being Conscious? Until, of course, life-altering experiences change your paradigm significantly. Everything changes. You begin to become Conscious. What a concept!

I had a remarkable life. I was married 22 years. From that outward perspective, my life did appear normal. That was an accomplishment in itself. In retrospect, my marriage taught me so much about my Self. When I got married, it was expected. As the child that I was, when my friends would talk about getting married and having children, it didn't resonate with me. Although I did go along with the program.

This was the Consciousness in which I was raised. I am not judging it, but I did play by the plan that society at that time told me how my life should be. I had my first near death experience in December 1965. When this occurred, it was very difficult to talk about what had happened to me. I kept it to my Self, knowing that no one at the time would understand my experience. I knew intuitively that my life was changing, regardless of the linear time it would take before it emerged to my surface Consciousness.

By all accounts and purposes, I should have been dead! In a new 1965 Corvette, I was hit twice by another car and thrown up over a curb, cutting down a 40-foot evergreen tree and going through a cement block wall. Metaphorically, this would have meaning to me many years later. In my first book, *The Age of Inheritance*, there is a section on breaking through the eight block wall. Since everything happens for a reason, it is now reasonable to me why it happened. How telling was that experience to my future!

From entrepreneur to corporate America, my career evolved. Changing careers on a regular basis was part of my journey. I would get bored, although I loved everything I did and learned. I loved changing what I did even more. So the changes occurred.

One of my favorite learning was flying airplanes. I belonged to the Ninety Nines, the International Organization of Women Pilots. I was very involved in aviation, in all aspects including air shows, volunteering at aviation museums, and lecturing. This was a memory that is one of my best times.

In retrospect, I know why I loved flying so much…I was above it all! I could look down and not be caught up in the daily trauma dramas. I was free. Probably the only times I was truly grounded to the earth was when I was flying. Whether I was flying an airplane or flying out of body, it was the same to me. An escape!

Memorial Day weekend, 1991, I had my second near death experience. I was helping a drunken woman get her car out of a parking space by getting into the car my Self. The car took off with me, accelerating from 0 to 60. The car flew 40 feet into the air, landing upside down in the Connecticut River in 15 feet of water. What a flying experience!

Before the car hit the water, I was out of my body, which of course is not unusual for me. Escaping, I thought I had really done it this time. In the No-Time (non-linear time), I was sitting on a ship in a white room with twelve wondrous all white Beings who spoke emphatically to me. I was "feeling" them. I was the only Being in the room in color. I was wearing a black and white knit jacket piped in red, with a matching top with an anchor on it. How appropriate!

In our conversation, the Beings expressed to me that I had made an agreement to go back to Earth to assist others in their healing process. "What agreement?" I asked. I didn't want to go back. Through the window of the ship, I could see all the commotion that was going on around the marina in Old Saybrook, Connecticut. I knew I would go back. I knew what they were saying was my Truth. But I fought it because it was not what I wanted. Although I knew that I had agreed. Back to Earth.

My life has never been the same. Since then, it's been a series of never-ending changes, upheavals, and even transformations. My life is totally devoted to the QuantumPathic® Center of Consciousness and to the QuantumPathic® Energy Method that I created to support individuals to heal their Selves. One of the significant reasons, and there were many, that I returned to Earth is to heal my Self and to figure out why I created the "good" and the "bad" in my life! And in the process, my total focus became my passion to assist my clients and students to empower their Selves and to comprehend how to heal their Selves. Through their Self-healing, they take charge of their own lives and deliberately create their lives from their Inner Truth while letting go of the Duality Fear Programs.

I do not call my Self a teacher or healer but a facilitator for others. I support others to go to their quantum cellular level of Consciousness, learn the Truth of who they are, and take back their Power and their life. By releasing the old fear patterns and programming, their lives change automatically. It is through their dedication and commitment to their Selves that I can support them through their Conscious healing process.

I am in love with what I do. I am living my purposes. This is my reason for living, staying, and loving this planet. It can't get any better than that! And so it is for me!

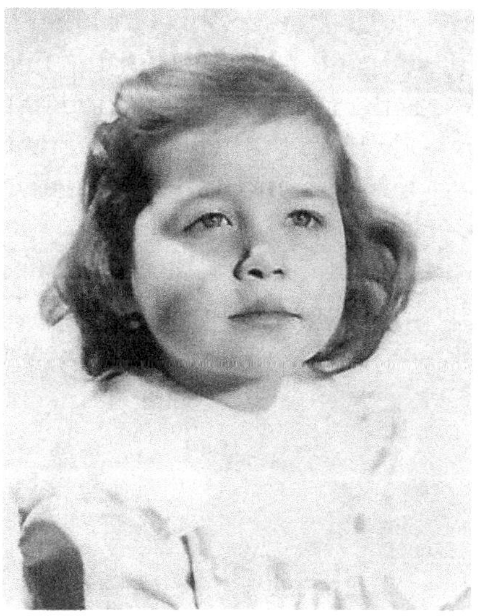

On my refrigerator, I have this picture of me at three. It is so evident from my eyes that I was not grounded to this earth plane, but rather living somewhere else. There is a saying that the eyes are the windows to the Soul. No doubt from this picture, what was going on inside of me was very different than my outside life. My eyes tell it all.

"I live my dream in realness. My bliss is to show you how to live your dream in realness. There is no greater joy for me than to witness my students and clients connect to themselves, to their bodies, perhaps for the first time, and to see them released from the grip of their past and become truly present and free."

Sherry Anshara is a medical intuitive, author, teacher, professional speaker, and founder of the QuantumPathic® Center of Consciousness in Scottsdale, Arizona and the online QuantumPathic® Institute. She has become known as "The Consciousness Expert".

She is the creator of the QuantumPathic® Energy Method (QPEM), which is a tool set people can implement to heal their Selves physically, mentally, emotionally, spiritually, and financially by accessing their Cellular Memory to get to the root cause of their traumas and issues and release it. For the first time, this progressive process is the practical connection of Consciousness within the human body from the cellular level that blends together all aspects of life — business, medicine, alternative healthcare, quantum physics, science, and relationships — into the Allness of the Multi-Dimensional Self. She attributes the successful results of the QuantumPathic® Energy Method to the intelligence of the body and its innate impulse towards health and well-being.

Other books written by Sherry Anshara:

The Age of Inheritance: The Activation of the 13 Chakras
And the Point Is…? Beyond Duality
Glossary of QuantumPathic® Terms: How to Understand the Quantum Energy of Human Life
Take Back Your Power: You Becoming You
Depression Doesn't Have to Leave You Depressed (e-book)
Getting Your Answers in 10 Minutes or Less (e-book)

Meditation CD's by Sherry Anshara:

Awakening the Divine Being Within Yourself
Beyond the Seven Chakra System
Clear Conscious Meditation
Expanding Your Awareness
Opening Your Heart Chakra and Speaking Your Truth
Total Relaxation Meditation

Glossary

Allness: Allness is a significant factor of Clear Consciousness as you shift out of Duality. Without judging Oneness, which makes everyone the same, Allness allows you to recognize and acknowledge your uniqueness and the uniqueness of all life in this Universe and the Multi-verses and *feel* the connection to all life without the Duality burden of sameness. Allness honors uniqueness.

Belief Systems: These are the ideas, concepts, and core beliefs acquired, consciously or unconsciously, throughout your time continuum. Creating your life from Duality's Belief Systems is not creating your life consciously. It is actualizing your life through someone else's or some group's opinion. Duality's Fear-based Belief Systems "support" you to be limited by hindering your unlimited Creative Power.

Cellular Memorization: This is the composite of the memorized information in your cells via the conditioning of ideas, Belief Systems, concepts, etc. in this current lifetime.

Cellular Memory: This is the composite of information from all of your experiences in your time continuum, stored in the cells in your body.

Childish Adult Ego (CAE): Your Childish Adult Ego lives through your Script until you are willing to let go of the programs and create your life consciously. Your CAE is the master of manipulation and control. He/She is stuck in the past, struggles to be validated, and wanty-needy's to be "right".

Wherever your CAE is stuck in the past at the various ages of the traumas and the dramas, this is the place or places from where your CAE is running your life, regardless of your current age and time frame.

This planet is run by Childish Adult Egos demanding to be right. It is long overdue for everyone's CAE to grow up and move beyond Duality and the Third Dimension on this planet.

Choice/Choose: As a Non-Emotional Observer and a Conscious Creator, you are In Charge of your Life. No matter what the scenario or condition, you comprehend without doubt that you have choices and options. You can choose differently or not. As the observer, you realize with *real eyes* that you are not bound by the old Duality Programming.

Completion: Completion is both the Newness of Non-Duality and the finale of Duality. In the Clear Consciousness of completion, you can be finished with Self-Judgment, Judgment of others, and Lack in all forms, and there is no sane reason to be caught up in the Take-Away dualistic Karma, Lessons, and Re-incarnation Programs. Be DONE!

Consciousness: Consciousness is awareness. However, you can be aware without being fully Conscious. There are various degrees or different spaces of Consciousness. The more Conscious you are, the deeper the level of comprehension you have about a situation, issue, or person.

Contract: Contracts are the carefully crafted outlines, physically and metaphorically written in Duality, which are supposed to teach you your Lessons, Karma, and Re-incarnation agendas. Through your contracts, the objective is to "ascend" your Self above your emotional and physical attachments to your past(s). In Duality, your contracts are the binds or handcuffs that keep you stuck in the re-cycle bins of your left computer/brain's Duality Fear Programs of Self-Judgment, Lack, and Take-Away. The scenes, clothes, times, and gender may change, but your Role, your Behaviors, and your emotional attachments to your Duality Profiles keep you stuck in the Duality loops of infinity.

Control: Control is a dysfunctional Duality Program that is based upon force. It is based upon forcing your Self or someone else to comply within the framework of a limited Belief System that does not support life to be lived freely and creatively. Control has no flexibility. Control takes away your personal Power.

Decision: When the Fear Programs are ingrained in you, you think you do not have options and choices to empower your Self.

You make decisions through fear-based programming which limit your options. Instead of consciously creating your Real desires, you settle by selecting one of the very limited options which have been created *outside* of you, and not by you.

Duality: Duality is the Belief Systems based upon only two decisions (no choices) of participation on this planet Earth: either right or wrong, black or white, have or have not, victim or victimizer, abuser or abusee, etc. Duality is limitations of every kind. There is no room for negotiation. A hierarchy is the rule of thumb; there is only a winner or a loser.

Duality is manipulated perceptions without facts – all true but not always the Truth. When one is living through perceptions not based on facts, one is easy to control and easy to manipulate.

Frequency: Frequency is a wavelength of energy or a band which is either emitted from Duality's limited Belief Systems or the Clear Unlimited Consciousness from within you. Whatever frequency you are emitting becomes either your Law of Distraction-Attraction or your clear Law of Attraction.

Whatever wavelength you are on, either from Duality or Non-Duality, you become connected to your outside world, which includes individuals and groups. What you choose is the wavelength from which you create your life.

Heartness: Your Heart is the most expanded frequency and vibration field in your body when you are consciously creating and living in the moment. Heartness is the Unconditional Love essence within you. Heartness is timeless beyond Duality.

In Charge: In Charge is your ability as the Non-Emotional Observer to see life through the facts and not the emotional conditions that suppress your freedom and your creativity. When you are in charge of your life, you have all the facts, you can make clear choices instead of emotional decisions, and your life flows fearlessly. You have a clear, deep sense of your own personal empowerment to be who you are.

Non-Emotional Observer (NEO): As the Non-Emotional Observer, you can observe from a viewpoint of the facts, and not from emotional attachments to previous experiences or repetitive experiences. As NEO, you support your Self to see not only how you are participating in a situation but also the participations of the other individual(s) who are in your life. As NEO, you can begin to see clearly the aspects or components of your own behavior, the repeated, dysfunctional Profiles you attract into your life, and the repeated Roles you have played out in your situations, conditions, and experiences. As the Non-Emotional Observer, you free your Self from being controlled and manipulated, and you stop controlling and manipulating your Self back into repeated patterns that do not serve you. You are in your Power.

Perfect Child Within (PCW): The Perfect Child Within is your natural, inherent Christed Consciousness of unlimitedness. Your Perfect Child Within is the activator of your 13 Chakras.

Profiles: A Profile is not one person. It is a label for an aspect of people that you have been conditioned or programmed to accept in your life. Profiles are the subjective labels you place on them, including your Self, when you put them in boxes with unrealistic emotional expectations of how the relationships are supposed to be according to the limitations of Duality.

Here is an example of a Victim Profile. If you are programmed to be a victim, then you must dysfunctionally attract a Victimizer Profile to you. It does not matter about gender. It is the frequency and vibration of the Profile with which you have been programmed to resonate.

Programming: Programming is related to ongoing exposure, repetition, training, and encoding in Duality. Consciously or unconsciously, your Belief Systems are "programmed" into your Consciousness.

QuantumPathic® Energy Method: The QuantumPathic® Energy Method is a practical, integrative tool utilizing guidance, language, visualization, and healing techniques, which supports you to get to the core of your issues — emotionally, mentally, physically, spiritually, and financially — in 10 minutes or less for a resolution at the cellular memory level of your Consciousness. There are no solutions without resolution. The QuantumPathic® Energy Method is the path to resolutions, without the concept that healing takes a long time or has to be expensive. In medicine, quantum physics, and psychology/psychiatry it is called Psychoneuroimmunology; in religion and metaphysics it is called healing; in your life it is called RESULTS to live the life that you require, desire, and deserve.

Real/Realness: Without illusions or delusions, Realness is the Truth of your Clear Consciousness.

Reality/Realities: Realities are Duality's versions of the illusions or delusions.

Roles: These are labels assigned to you from the beginning of you in your current and past lives, whether you resonate to them or not. Most of the time, you are placed in labeled boxes, preventing you from being the Truth of you. You get caught up in these Roles, trying, trying, and trying to *fit in.* You and many will say, "I always felt different." Out of the Duality Reality, you can let go of the assigned Roles that do not fit you.

Thinky-Thinky: When you are in your head/computer brain, your brain has no idea what time it is. As you stay in your left computer/brain, you get stuck in your brain's neuro-nets in a non-productive experience, situation, or event that happened 98% of the time the past. The 2% of the turmoil of the thinky-thinky occurs when you are projecting into a future that has not occurred yet. Your left computer/brain thinky-thinkys over and over again about the past and even about the possible future event that has no relationship to your present moment.

The results of thinky-thinky include not being able to go to sleep at night, not connected to your body, or out-of-body situations of being completely ungrounded. In the frequency and vibration of thinky-thinky, you are not in the current moment. Your left computer/brain is projecting you somewhere else. It doesn't matter whether it is the past or the future. Your body has to go along with your emotional thinky-thinky. It does not matter in what time frame you are caught, you cannot have clear thoughts. You can only have a turmoil of neuro-nets running through your left computer/brain non-effectively and non-efficiently. Thinky-thinky prevents you from being in the current moment.

Vibration: Vibration is the energy being emitted or given off by a person, place, or situation. Vibrations are *felt* and are communicated through your feelings, consciously or unconsciously. These feelings are communicated from you to another person or group, and vice versa.

Vibrations can feel great or they can feel debilitating and frightening. Trusting your intuition is a great guide. If something or someone does not *feel* correct to you, your vibrations are not compatible.

Wanty-Needy: The frequency and vibration of wanty-needy is the dysfunctional behavior of craving, wishing, and hoping to be loved. The wanty-needy resonance is powerless. It keeps you looking outside of your Self for love. To release this low-based, wanty-needy resonance, the first step is loving your Self unconditionally and accepting you are lovable regardless of anyone else's opinion. Replace the wanty-needy resonance with *Require! Require* is an action word. It has a resonance of empowerment. Wanty-needy has no empowerment to offer. Wanty-needy is the resonance of a victim.

There are no solutions without a resolution…

The QuantumPathic® Energy Method
is the path to resolutions.

QuantumPathic® Center of Consciousness
6701 E. Clinton St., Scottsdale, AZ 85254
(480) 609-0874

www.QuantumPathic.com
www.SherryAnshara.com
www.QuantumPathicInstitute.com
www.youtube.com/quantumpathic

Made in the USA
Monee, IL
24 January 2024